C000194351

TOGETHER F

According to authors Sue and Khalil Khavari, a successful lifelong marriage is within everyone's grasp. In this practical yet inspiring book, topics of discussion include preparing oneself for marriage and attracting the right mate, the importance of compatibility and complementarity in a relationship, and how to keep open the lines of communication. They offer tips on how to handle each partner's emotions, manage financial matters, deal with relatives, and avoid the common traps that threaten even the most secure of relationships.

Written in a down-to-earth style with many everyday examples, *Together Forever* offers an encouraging, optimistic approach to the difficult but immensely rewarding task of nurturing life's most precious relationship – that between husband and wife.

About the Authors

KHALIL A. KHAVARI is Professor of Psychology at the University of Wisconsin-Milwaukee. He has served as Director of the University's Conflict Resolution and Peace Studies Program. The author of many articles in the fields of psychology and conflict resolution, he and his wife Sue have co-authored *Creating a Successful Family*, also published by Oneworld.

SUE WILLISTON KHAVARI received her Master's degree in Library and Information Science in 1972 and subsequently served as the Director of Technical Services at the Law School Library of Marquette University until 1985. She now works as a freelance writer. She and Khalil have two adult children.

Dedication

To all successful lifelong marriages – especially yours

TOGETHER FOREVER

A Handbook for Creating a Successful Marriage

Khalil A. Khavari, Ph.D.

&

Sue Williston Khavari, M.A.

ONEWORLD
OXFORD

Together Forever

Oneworld Publications Ltd
(Sales and Editorial)
185 Banbury Road, Oxford, OX2 7AR, England

Oneworld Publications Ltd
(U.S. Sales Office)
County Route 9, P.O. Box 357
Chatham, NY 12037, USA

© Khalil and Sue Khavari 1993
All rights reserved. Copyright under Berne Convention

A CIP record for this book is available from the British Library

ISBN 1-85168-061-6

Printed and bound in Great Britain
by the Guernsey Press Co. Ltd.,
Guernsey, Channel Islands

CONTENTS

PREFACE

Our research and personal experience lead us to the view that marriage can serve men and women in ways that no other arrangement can match. For marriage to live up to its potential, however, requires dedication to its success and the willingness to do the work.

A marriage is a living organism. It needs nourishment, care and protection to make it thrive – and work at full vitality. This book is for people who believe in the worth of marriage and are willing to learn new skills, apply them, and enjoy the rewards of their joint labor.

Marriage, a uniquely human practice, is thought to be well over 100,000 years old. The endurance and universality of marriage are solid proofs of its worth, and show its resilience – the ability to accommodate social and cultural changes among diverse human societies and across the ages.

A successful marriage that will satisfy your needs and brings you happiness is of vital importance because no other success can make up for an unhappy personal life. When our home life is satisfying and energizing, we are much better able to handle outside troubles.

Marriage is a paradox; two very different people optimistically invest themselves in a mutual venture. In the past, there were fewer risks of failure because people married within their own social group and the wife was traditionally dominated and absorbed by the husband. In modern marriages, however, the partners are equal and frequently come from different social, cultural, racial or religious backgrounds. The challenge, then, is to harmonize their different, yet equally valid, characteristics.

The task facing the modern marriage is to respect the unique qualities that make the two partners different, while achieving compatibility. When this happens, we have a richness that can be created only by the harmonizing of differences. After all, you would never want to marry your own clone – as wonderful as you may be. You would be bored and incomplete. You want to marry someone who is beautifully different, yet fully compatible.

When two people marry, they do more than simply share their previously separate lives. They create a new entity – not unlike giving birth to a child. It is an entity that governs their lives and has a personality of its own. To make yours the best possible marriage, you need to know certain things not only about your spouse, but also about yourself. You need to know how you and your partner can accommodate the requirements of this new entity – marriage – for the benefit of the two of you.

If you are already married, this book will help you make your marriage live up to its fullest potential. If you are thinking about getting married, whether for the first time or not, it will give you the information you need to go about it intelligently – following your heart while using your head.

We thank Juliet Mabey and Novin Doostdar for their unfailing support. We also are grateful to Jan Nikolic for her excellent editorial assistance. Finally, we owe a debt of gratitude to all the people who have contributed either directly or indirectly to the substance of this book.

Khalil A. Khavari
Sue Williston Khavari
Milwaukee, Wisconsin
January, 1993

PART one

RETHINKING MARRIAGE

A great deal of turmoil surrounds marriage. Some believe that it is an obsolete practice, others find it unsatisfying and try different arrangements – yet many enter into it with great hopes.

In this section, we discuss issues that are central to the success of marriage – and provide advice on how to deal with them. Concerns such as changing social and cultural practices, the demands of modern life, and the reconciling of seemingly contradictory positions are addressed. We make a case for rethinking marriage – to make it responsive to the needs of the couple. Every aspect of life is rapidly changing, and marriage should not resist this universal trend. It can and it should welcome change and continue to meet the needs of the pair bonded for a lifelong marriage.

▶ 1 ◀

CHAPTER

OLD & NEW WAYS OF THINKING

An elderly couple walked hand in hand along the edge of a meadow golden in the late afternoon light. They watched with fascination as a pair of birds were wheeling, swooping, and exploring high in the boundless blue sky. At all times, each bird was independent, yet acutely aware of the other. While permitting plenty of wing space to fly safely, they never allowed too much distance to come between them.

Far below, the woman squeezed the man's hand and said, "That's us, dear. That's the way we have been – always close, but never crowding each other." He gently responded, "Yes, ours has been a life of companionship. An emotional, intellectual and physical bond. We have been like one person disguised as two." They smiled into each other's eyes with a love that had lasted throughout their lives and would continue to the end of time.

The above episode actually happened. And, with enough effort and wisdom, it can happen to you. As you read these pages, a variation of the same theme is being played ali over the world. Marriage can be the most marvelous of all human relationships, and it is possible to make yours one of the many lifelong successful marriages.

It has been said that ideas have consequences. We live what we think and we think what we live. It is important to keep this mind–action relationship responsive to healthy changes. We can't insist on old ways that no longer work. So rethinking and adjusting our actions accordingly are at the heart of human progress in all spheres of life. And marriage is no exception; this rethinking of marriage has to be done right at the start. That is, the couple must build their relationship on the solid foundation of modern thinking. Then, they need to remain flexible – nurturing the ability to adjust, to make necessary changes – as their life of togetherness encounters new demands, opportunities and circumstances.

GENDER ROLES AND CUSTOMS

While as a species we are willing to rethink things and change our ways, we also value stability. Consequently, we think many things through, reach a satisfactory conclusion, and form laws and rules for our social behaviour. Once we make these rules, we tend to resist changing them. Then rules we made ourselves begin ruling us. Some rules are formal, while others emerge informally. Marriage – a social activity – is heavily regulated by both laws and customs. Customs evolve gradually and give way to change only grudgingly. From time to time, pressure for change builds and forces a major reorganization of society's cherished ways – when the prevailing customs or cultural practices become incapable of incorporating new ideas and practices. When this happens in science, it is called a 'paradigm shift'.[1]

We believe that human culture is currently experiencing a paradigm shift – many of the old rules and practices have become useless, and a comprehensive rethinking is needed to meet the requirements of the time. The obsolescence of the old ideas is glaringly apparent in the area of gender role and marriage. For centuries, societies lived by the rule of gender, defining different functions and expectations for the two sexes. But times have changed.

Decades ago, the famed anthropologist Margaret Mead documented the fact that gender roles are socially determined, not sex-linked. All human societies had adopted and promoted gender roles – some more strict than others. This is the old paradigm (see Table). At its heart has been the assumption of male superiority and dominance – perhaps as a result of the value that was placed on physical strength. These gender roles are drilled into children early and strictly enforced throughout life, and those wilful boys and girls who attempt to refuse their assigned roles are usually subjected to unrelenting pressure to conform.

Table 1. A partial list of gender roles and stereotypes for men and women under the old paradigm.

MEN	WOMEN
Rational	Emotional
Tough	Delicate and tender
Dominant	Submissive
Strong	Weak
Aggressive	Tame and docile
Competitive	Cooperative
Brave	Timid
Contemplative, reserved	Talkative
Achiever	Complacent
Just	Compassionate
Assertive	Retiring
Patient	Impulsive
Wise	Immature
Breadwinner	Homemaker
Active, no nonsense	Passive, sweet
Mathematical	Verbal
Physical	Non-physical
Hunting	Cooking, sewing

Freud was wrong when he said anatomy determines destiny, in a reference to the different roles of men and women; he was articulating the prevailing mentality of the old paradigm. The anatomical difference between men and women is insignificant compared with all that the two sexes share in common –

cognition, emotion, spirituality, creativity, and the entire spectrum of human nature.

Much of what we know about marriage and what men and women are like is learned haphazardly. We form our ideas by observing our parents, grandparents, or friends; from television, movies and what we read; and from our own imagination. The media, for example, often portray women's role as that of pleasing men and having babies. Women are shown standing about watching men do things – often with great admiration and even awe; they are seldom shown with any ambitions of their own.

The new paradigm, in contrast to the old, is not only egalitarian, it is free from stereotyping. It is dynamic and responsive to change in the unique circumstances of a given couple. It does not use a broad brush to paint people on the basis of gender. Don't let your marriage get trapped in the awful web of obsolescent tradition. The two of you decide on your joint life agenda with an eye to what each of you wants to do rather than what others want you to do. Our advice is to scrap the idea of gender roles altogether.

In the past, the power of tradition guided females and males along different paths – girls were steered along the domestic path while boys were guided on the external path.

- *Women and the domestic path.* The domestic path has its own agenda. Girls have dolls, play house, care for babies, do dishes, wash, clean, mend, and cook. The goal of the domestic path was attainment of *womanhood*, as defined by *wifehood* and *motherhood*. Essentially, this marked the end of the trail for most women – being a wife and a mother was the culmination of their aspirations. Only a few women were able to go beyond this limit and attain some degree of *personhood* – the realm of fulfillment and achievement beyond domesticity.
- *Men and the external path.* The external path, into which boys were channeled, also has its program. Boys play war games, pose as warriors, knights, and leaders of society. They are the hunters, the braves and the chiefs. Boys were also directed toward a *manhood* that included *husbandhood*

and *fatherhood*, yet, boys could go beyond manhood to *personhood* without having to fulfill the role of husband or father.

These outdated cultural practices that confine people to certain paths have no place in the new paradigm. Gender should not be the sole basis for limitations or opportunities. Traditions are the habits of the group, and like personal habits, they die hard. Many people still tenaciously cling to old traditions, while others pick and choose from the old and the new as it suits them. But a major break with the past is the requirement of the new social paradigm.

Traditionally, women have tended to 'marry up' and men have 'married down'. That is, women have wanted to choose husbands who were not only older than themselves, but their superior in social, economic, and educational terms. Male dominance in the past was partly due to an unequal arrangement where women, who have always had the same range of intellectual ability as men, were not permitted to develop their potential and were made subservient to men. Today, women are increasingly receiving the same educational and work opportunities as men, and this will bring about a more equal marriage partnership.

"To live by role expectations seems consistently in opposition to a marriage which is going somewhere, which is in process. . . . So in the only marriages which seem enriching and satisfying roles play a lesser and lesser part."[2]

THE NEW MARRIAGE PARADIGM

Marriage, in one form or another, has been around nearly as long as humanity itself.[3] With remarkable resilience, the practice of marriage has adapted itself to meet the requirements of different times and places. In our view, we are presently witnessing a major change in the rules and practice of marriage, and a new model of marriage is replacing outdated conceptions.

The modern framework for marriage is based on the realization that recent changes in all facets of human relationships require a new set of rules and guidelines – a paradigm shift – to make marriage work. The modern marriage paradigm is based on an equal partnership between the husband and the wife. It is free of gender stereotypes, and both partners equally share the work as well as the fruits of their efforts. We agree with Bertrand Russell, who said: "There was, I think, never any reason to believe in any innate superiority of the male, except his superior muscle." Some contrasting features of the old and the new paradigm are highlighted below.

- Modern life with its labor-saving devices has freed the wife from limitations traditionally imposed by household chores. Simultaneously, the sole-provider husband is rapidly disappearing. The new marriage paradigm is a joint venture of two different, yet equal, partners.
- There has long been the mistaken assumption that there are fundamental biological differences between men and women. Now science tells us that of the 100,000 genes that go into the making of a man or a woman only one gene, on chromosome #4, is responsible for the determination of gender. All the others we share as human beings.[4] Even psychological and behavioral differences between the two genders are largely the products of cultural practices.
- Under the old paradigm women were objects of worship, seen as pure, innocent, childlike, in need of protection, emotional, and so forth. In the new paradigm, there is no place for such unwarranted suppositions. Why should women be objects of worship just by virtue of their gender? Humans – men and women alike – are subject to all the human frailties, weaknesses, and faults. Humans are loved in spite of these flaws, not because they are perfect.
- In the old paradigm the husband took on the dominant role – establishing himself as the law, the last word, supreme. Husbands assumed a paternal attitude toward their wives, who were frequently younger, less well-educated, relegated to subservient roles, and financially dependent. In the new paradigm, girls and boys have equal opportunities for developing their natural abilities, social repression of females is less severe, and each partner brings definite assets to the marriage.

● In the old paradigm where men were appointed as the law givers, women were designated as the affection givers. Women frequently 'mothered' their husbands – because of the men's immaturity, women's need to fulfill the motherhood role, or as an indirect way of dominating the husband. In the modern paradigm, no mothering or fathering of a spouse is acceptable. Instead, there is nurturing of each other as two adults sharing their gifts for the benefit of both. The relationship is based on the win–win principle – where both husband and wife always come out winners – and not the zero-sum strategy where one person's gain is always at another's expense. When both gain, the marriage gains; and when the marriage gains, humanity benefits. Henry Ford was among the first to recognize the value of the win–win relationship. He shocked his contemporary industrialists by raising the wage of a worker to the then astronomical figure of $5 per hour. He correctly reasoned that well-paid workers work harder, are happier with their job, are more likely to stay with the company, and can afford to buy automobiles. This practice, in turn, increased workers' productivity, sales, and profits.

● In the old paradigm, the struggle for domination was central to many marriages. In most cases, the wife was defeated early on, if she dared to put up any struggle. Women's defeat was virtually assured, since men held most power. In some instances, the struggle became a permanent fixture of marriage, resulting in many years of pitched battles.

● Under the new paradigm women get married without the traditional social and financial pressures. It is strictly an optional decision for them. Hence, the pressure to get married in the first place and to stay in a bad marriage at all costs is no longer as all-pervasive as it once was, and men must make marriage more appealing for women in order to attract them and keep them.

● In the new paradigm, parity, friendship and respect is the norm. Each spouse not only avoids any action that stifles the other, but will do all he or she can to nurture the other. In the new paradigm, the relationship is level, healthy and stable – the two partners are shoulder-to-shoulder, pulling together in the same direction.

● Central to the new paradigm is devotion to enlightened self-interest. For instance, when you are supportive to your spouse, when you do something nice and make him or her feel good, you are acting in your own self-interest, because all your good deeds will generate compounded benefits that sooner or later will revert back to you. Similarly, anything you do that harms your spouse – even if it seems to serve your immediate, short-term goals – is ultimately detrimental to you too.

● The new paradigm requires not only tolerating individual differences, it demands respect and even encouragement of differences between the partners. Differences, and even conflicts, are not inherently bad or destructive. They can be a source of excitement and enrichment. The new paradigm is about accommodation and mutual appreciation. It is about learning how to create unity in diversity.

● In the new rethinking, there is the realization that sharing power is gaining – not losing – power. When men share their traditional *macropower* – the power of making the important decisions on the external path – they automatically surrender with it some of their responsibilities. Women use that power for the benefit of the union. Similarly, when women give up some of their *micropower* – the power associated with the internal path – they also empower their husbands and relieve themselves of sole responsibility for the home. When couples share power, satisfaction with marriage is high.[5]

● The new paradigm is about mutual respect and compatibility – the pillars of any successful relationship.

COHABITATION

Inability to rethink marriage and make it responsive to the requirements of the time has led some to experiment with other arrangements. Living together without being married – cohabiting – is an instance. It has gone from being stigmatized in the twenties, to risqué in the thirties and forties, to commonplace since the seventies. We don't think much of cohabitation. And our disapproval is not based strictly on moral grounds. Here are some of the reasons why cohabitation is not a good idea.

● *Hesitation and casualness.* Moving in with someone without marrying the person indicates a casual approach and a hesitation in making a permanent commitment to the relationship. It is somewhat like buying an appliance on a home-trial basis. It lacks that vital ingredient of really wanting the person for life and the willingness to do it right and for keeps.

● *Temporary relationship.* Most live-in arrangements never lead to marriage. Only nineteen percent of cohabiting men marry the woman they are living with.[6] People who really want to be married shouldn't think that the way to it is through cohabitation.

● *Higher divorce rate.* Many cohabitators reason that by living together, they'll have a chance to find out if they really want to make a permanent relationship out of it. So, when they get married, their marriage will last. Not so. The divorce rate is 80 percent higher among people who had lived together before marriage than those who had not.

● *Differences in motives.* Men, as a general rule, cohabit for sex while women cohabit for commitment and emotional bonding. This fundamental difference in motivation adds greatly to the unsatisfactory nature of cohabitation. This sort of relationship is not a mature, balanced, and mutually fulfilling arrangement.

● *Female victimization.* A number of studies have shown that live-in arrangements largely favor men in many ways. Cohabiting men are much more promiscuous than women and expose their partners to contracted venereal disease, for instance. The men are also less likely to do their equal share of household work. Further, they tend to move more readily to another partner and they are less considerate than husbands are.[6] Wife abuse is a tragic feature of a bad marriage, but the incidence of battered women is even greater among cohabiting than married couples.[7]

● *Break-up pain.* Studies show that break-up of live-in arrangements is as traumatic as divorce. There is nothing really temporary or carefree about cohabiting. The only ingredient lacking is the very vital one that makes for successful relationships – the commitment to love that very special person for life. When break-up comes, there is heartache, legal battles, and almost all the ingredients of divorce.

● *Low satisfaction.* Cohabiting couples have the lowest love and satisfaction scores relative to other forms of relationships.[8]

MARRIAGE AS A SOCIAL CONTRACT

Marriage is not just an arrangement of convenience – a way for two people to enjoy each other's gifts while it suits them and as long as nothing better comes along. People enter friendship with the expectation of forming a satisfying relationship. It is only an expectation, a hope. If it works out, fine. If it gets better, then great. If it doesn't work out, the parties will go their own ways with no major harm done. Usually, there is no prior commitment on the part of either party that the friendship they are hoping to form will last to the end of time.

In marriage, on the other hand, there must be a conviction, a commitment from the start that the relationship is good, that it will get better, and that it is for keeps. The try and see attitude has no place in marriage. Because that, in itself, will undermine the determination and the commitment to make it the very best and lasting relationship possible. Marriage should not be entered into with the idea of till divorce us do part.

This is one reason why cohabitation, trial marriages, and other forms of pre-marriage intimacy are bad ideas to begin with. They have a large element of hesitancy, trepidation, and leaving an escape hatch. Marriage is a total commitment and that is the only way that it is going to be successful. The only two alternative thoughts in marriage have to be: it will either succeed or it will succeed! This commitment together with the willingness to do the work in an atmosphere of equality, respect and love make for a successful marriage.

▶ 2 ◀

CHAPTER

FUNDAMENTAL CONCEPTS ABOUT MARRIAGE

An eastern adage says: "Twin blessings ordinarily go unnoticed, until we lose them. They are health and safety." We would like to expand on that by including the rest of our individual and collective blessings. With respect to marriage, a number of blessings that significantly affect the partners and society are not always clearly seen or appreciated. Some of them are listed here.

- *The union of a man and a woman in marriage is at the heart of a stable society*. The two essential ingredients of unity are compatibility and mutual respect. Unity releases energy, disunity saps and destroys it. People who are energized by a strong, stable and loving unity at home are much more likely to be able to work successfully with others outside the home – giving and receiving friendship and goodwill.
- *Marriage can be a 'fortress for well-being'*. Marriage can safeguard the couple's emotional and physical health. But this fortress is not handed out with the marriage license. It must be diligently built – stone by stone – through the cooperative labor of the couple. And a fortress, regardless of how well it has been built, is always in need of maintenance.

Work must continue to improve it, replace its worn-out parts, and further beautify it. The work demanded for the marital fortress recognizes no breaks, weekends, or holidays. Some of the work is exciting, much of it tolerable, and some is plain drudgery. Yet it all must be done to keep it in good repair – so that the fortress can withstand the assaults of the inevitable problems of life and furnish its owners with the full measure of its strong protection.

● *The partners as future parents.* To raise the children of the 21st century, all the talents and resources of two committed adults are needed. There is no shortage of human beings in the world; what is in short supply is resourceful and devoted parents who are willing to make the needed sacrifices for raising outstanding children. And the best environment for so doing is still the home – a home strongly anchored to a thriving marriage.

● *Marriage is not a business transaction, or simply a legal contract.* Being married to someone is not the same as holding the title on a property. A marriage certificate is not a license for possessiveness, abuse, or stifling the partner. The financial disadvantages of women place them in a subservient position. In the United States, for example, the average weekly earning for males is $500 and only $351 for females.[9] Marriage should be a charter for the exaltation of the partners, the children, and the flourishing of all those associated with it.

● *Marriage is no bed of roses.* Look closely and you will surely see all the thorns lurking under the alluring petals. Yet the partners can remove as many thorns as possible. It will be a lifelong job, but well worth it. Few couples ever succeed in getting rid of all the thorns. New thorns keep growing, and the pair must constantly work at removing them.

● *Marriage is compromise.* Compromising is the engine that propels the marriage toward an ever-increasing satisfaction and joy. Rigidity and selfishness work against compromise. They are the brakes that stop the marriage from growing and often derail it altogether.

● *Marriage is not a refuge for running away from problems.* Motivation to marry can be as varied as motivation for doing anything. Getting married to escape personal problems and personal unhappiness is seldom the solution.

● *Marriage is not submission.* Some people get married because they were pursued and talked into it. You shouldn't marry just to be agreeable and accommodating. Of course, it is flattering to have someone so interested in you that he or she wants to marry you. You should approach marriage with extreme care – trying to win for yourself the very best partner that you possibly can.

IMPORTANCE OF THE SPOUSE

In the past when people got married, the spouse was basically absorbed into an extended family. The family, friends, neighbors, and the town and village folks made up a stable core of a support system. Many people were related to each other; no one got married and moved away very far – they stayed put. Thus, in this fairly stable context the spouse was just another part – and not necessarily a very important one – in the person's support system.

Now, there is tremendous mobility. Job opportunities require frequent re-locations in distant places. Only a very small percentage of people live, grow old, and die in their birthplace community. This mobile society is highly impersonal. It is the type of anonymous society where everyone is a stranger, everyone is passing through. In this setting, a combination of mistrust, hesitancy in making friends that one may have to leave again, and fear of rejection make formation of new support systems difficult. Further, the couple's children usually leave home when they are still in their teens – for college, job, military service, or whatever. The empty-nest period can be the major part of life – many years of adulthood and retirement together, given the ever-increasing lifespan. These considerations demand that the couple be not only spouses to each other, but each other's best friend and support system. In the impersonal society of today, it is usually one's spouse who is the only constant in this ever-changing life, one's companion through thick and thin, and one's most valued partner.

Perhaps it is due to this increasingly important role of the spouse that some long-married people die shortly after the loss of their partner.[10] Hence, in the new paradigm, the spouse is a most significant person in your life – more so than children, parents or friends. The modern-day spouse is a dependable, loving provider of psychological and physical support in a highly impersonal world.

In the new paradigm, the marriage partner is very important for the following reasons.

● People are living much longer than they did only a few decades ago. A couple can reasonably expect to be married some 50 or more years. This is the most time one spends with another person. You want this time to be quality time. And it can be a lifelong experience of unique companionship.

● Change has become the constant of life. People are called upon to make all kinds of adjustments. Some examples are moving from one place to another; career and job changes; children coming into the home and leaving. And change, regardless of whether it is for the better or for the worse, is always jarring and stressful.[11] Hence, the stability of the relationship becomes even more important.

● The extended family and relatives – traditionally a vital core of support – are often in far away places, scattered, and cannot be relied upon. Most extended families come together briefly, if at all, at special occasions such as weddings and funerals. Correspondence and even telephone conversations are hardly satisfactory substitutes for the in-person, heart-to-heart intimacy that families of the past provided.

● Making life-long friends and keeping them is also a difficult and chancy thing – in part due to the highly mobile nature of modern society. Hence, relationships are often superficial. One's 'friends' are also in the same predicament. No one would want to invest the kind of time, energy and emotion that deep and meaningful relationships require when there is little assurance that the relationship will last for any length of time. The result is that people end up having many acquaintances and no real friends.

- The couple's children leave home, possibly to distant locations, when the pair is still in the prime of life – leaving them to each other, for the most part. It takes a strong bond to withstand the jarring shock of separation from the children. And when the children, in turn, marry, a second shock wave is felt. You are relegated to the periphery of their lives. You are happy for them. You wish them the very best. But you also feel the loss. It is the spouse – that faithful partner – who stays with you and who sustains you.
- In our more and more impersonal society, even neighbors of many years' standing are only superficial acquaintances. This is particularly true in affluent sprawling suburbia. They are called 'bedroom communities' because they lack all the ingredients that make for a neighborhood and neighborliness. One consequence is pervasive loneliness. Being lonely in the crowd is more than a literary expression; it is a fact of life.
- Traditional religious and social affiliations have also tended to become superficial – lacking in depth and failing to build caring relationships.

All the above and many other considerations combine to make the spouse more important than ever.

THE COUPLE AND MARRIAGE

Marriage is about two individuals who, together, create something superior to anything that either of them can produce alone. To do that, the couple must share their resources and energies with a clear vision. Otherwise they end up working at cross purposes, wasting energy, and creating a mess instead:

> We now know that the family is a unit in which all individuals have an important influence – whether they like it or not. The family is an interacting communications network in which every member from the day-old baby to the seventy-year-old grandmother influences the nature of the entire system and in turn is influenced by it. For example, if someone in the

> family feels ill, another member may function more effectively than he usually does. The system tends, by nature, to keep itself in balance. An unusual action by one member invariably results in a compensating reaction by another member. If mother hates to take Sunday drives but hides this feeling from her husband, the message is nevertheless somehow broadcast throughout the family communication network, and it may be Johnny, the four-year-old, who becomes 'carsick' and ruins the Sunday drive.[12]

People are highly interactive – we react to other human beings, objects, and situations. What a wife does importantly influences the reaction of her husband and vice versa. An ancient astronomer said, "Heaven is more than the stars alone. It is the stars and their movements." Everything in marriage, both good and bad, is a joint creation and property. Whatever the quality of the emotional atmosphere, it is always a shared responsibility.

YOKED MARRIAGES

We have high but realistic expectations about marriage. We believe that every marriage can become an outstanding relationship, if the couple follow certain rules and practices. Unfortunately many marriages are far from the success that they can be. A marriage, for instance, may be held together by the yoke of circumstances. The husband and the wife have some things in common, but not the full sharing of each other. The husband has his own universe – his job, friends, ambitions, hobbies, and so on. The wife is in another universe with her own preoccupations – trying to play her gender role as a mother, a homemaker, or a professional person in her own right. Ties such as children, financial and social considerations may play their roles in holding these marriages together. Any change – for example, children growing up and leaving home, or the wife getting a job and becoming financially independent – may be enough to end the relationship altogether.

This is an example of an empty marriage; a dream that got stalled; and an arrangement where neither partner has the sense, motivation or know-how to fix it, nor the courage to abort it: "In interviews with hundreds of average marital pairs we learned that approximately 80 percent of the couples had seriously considered divorce at one time or another, and many of them still think about it frequently. Often, only the existence of children, the restrictions of poverty, the edicts of religion, or a lack of courage blocks the decision to get divorced."[12]

Some experts have proposed that it takes just as much work to support a bad marriage as to support a good one. We believe that a bad marriage is even more costly in terms of time, energy, and emotions. We further believe that no one is doomed to a bad marriage, while everyone has the opportunity to make theirs the most rewarding venture of their lives. Having a good marriage is within everyone's grasp provided that they keep in mind the changing requirements of our time and behave accordingly. The next chapter considers the basic factors that make for a successful modern marriage.

▶ 3 ◀

CHAPTER

MODERN MARRIAGE

We said in the Preface that in our view marriage has the potential of serving the partners in ways that no other arrangement can match, if a couple shows dedication to its success and willingness to do the work. Part of that work is to retool both our thinking and our actions so that a relationship that has always nurtured humanity can continue to do so in the context of the modern age. Presently, marriages are in trouble the world over. Is it because, at long last, marriage has become obsolete? It is true that the old marriage paradigm has become non-functional and that modern requirements for marriage are fundamentally different in many ways. If we want a thriving marriage, we must adopt new practices.

REQUIREMENTS OF MODERN MARRIAGE

A modern marriage requires radical departure from many of the ways of thinking and the practices of the past. Central to the success of marriage is the realization that the docile woman of the past is hard to find; even if you find her, she is not likely to be the person you want to marry; and that a 'traditional' marriage is bound to fail – either ending up in divorce or operating considerably below its full potential. Some of the fundamental requirements of modern marriage are discussed below.

● *Gender equality*. Don't even let the thought enter your mind that you – by virtue of gender alone – are either superior or inferior. Traditionally, men have thought themselves superior and women felt subservient. This type of thinking is most destructive for the relationship. You are not identical, no two people ever are – not even identical twins; you are different, but equal. Realistically though, you may marry a person who still has a foot in the old world. He or she may not truly feel or believe in unconditional equality. Then, your task is to lovingly assist your partner to feel equal and to see the immense advantages that equality brings to the union.

● *Power equality*. With power goes responsibility; they are inseparable. Responsibility is the price for power. In modern marriage, equal sharing of power is the only smart thing to do. Neither husband nor wife should be the sole wielder of power. Power and responsibility should be equally shared, unless there are circumstances that make this impossible. For instance, if one spouse becomes incapacitated, then the other will have to take on greater power to meet the family's responsibilities. Otherwise, as tempting as it is, monopolizing power is a sure way of undermining a thriving and satisfying relationship. Of equal potential destructiveness is surrender of power to the partner.

● *Individuated bonding*. The partners in marriage are equal, but different. The two words that best capture the essence of a modern successful marriage – individuated bonding – sounds like a paradox. They stand for conditions that bring about the full flourishing of each partner as an independent human being, while simultaneously anchoring that personal expansion in a common bond. And there is nothing paradoxical about it. Each can strive to lead a full life of personal achievement without damaging the joint life of the couple. There must be compromises, to be sure, but compromise is not the same as sacrifice. In enlightened compromise, both parties gain. For a balance to be achieved, we propose you make it a rule to relinquish those personal freedoms that either of you feels may damage your mutual commitment. The decision to marry, in itself, is an instance of opting for mutual commitment over the personal freedom of single life.

● *Expansion, not assimilation.* The modern marriage demands expansion. The partners should be fully prepared for a broader life venture, where each is afforded the greatest possible opportunity to pursue legitimate aspirations. A marriage where a man gets himself a wife as just another acquisition, where she sacrifices all her personal aspirations that fall outside of wifehood and motherhood, where she is merely assimilated as another part in the husband's domain, is a relic of the past. This type of marriage rarely works today. Even when it seems to work, it is an anomaly.

ADVANTAGES OF BEING MARRIED

Some ask why get married at all. It is so much work and trouble. Our answer is that marriage is worth the trouble. The alternatives are not very attractive – staying single all one's life, never experiencing the joy of a permanently committed union; or shuttling in and out of relationships with all the attendant trauma. Would you really want to spend your life alone, without having someone to cherish, love, and care for? Without having someone to share your innermost thoughts and feelings through the years – the two of you passing from youth to old age together? Without someone who deeply loves and is concerned about you? Without having the opportunity to reciprocate? Whatever marriage costs, we think it easily wins over the competition.

As a rule, people abandon practices that don't work. Marriage is a practice that stood the test of time by proving its worth and by changing to meet new requirements.

After the Bolshevik Revolution, for example, the Communist government took steps to destroy marriage and the family, in its attempt to wipe out the old order. Marriage was demeaned; the ceremony became a mere formality performed in little offices by petty officials. Divorce was granted by simply presenting a statement of intention and paying a small fee. The government separated spouses by assigning them jobs in different towns. In 1927, a law was passed that made unregistered marriages as valid as registered ones. By 1932, family ties had eroded and social problems involving gangs and vandalism prevailed. Eventually, the State stopped recognizing unregistered marriages and ended its active campaign against marriage and the family.[13] It seems that marriage and the family are the bedrock of social order and stability, in addition to meeting numerous personal needs.[14]

Some of the advantages of marriage are listed below, and you can probably think of many more.

- *Solidarity*. A good marriage is worth working for. With a good marriage, illness, poverty, and other problems become bearable. The relationship of a man and a woman who are married is unique; there is a sense of trust and solidarity in each other. If one needs to let off steam or talk, the other is there. Couples cover and protect each other in all kinds of situations, and even when they have a quarrel, couples frequently abandon their argument and create solidarity in the presence of strangers.
- *Pooling of resources*. The pair can pool its income for a stronger financial base. In instances of job loss, physical or mental incapacity, and other misfortunes, there is a caring partner. The potential problems of old age can be handled more effectively when the two combine their resources.
- *Friendship*. Making friends is very difficult. Keeping them is even more taxing. In marriage, you have a permanent friendship, and one that is not likely to falter so easily.
- *Sharing*. The sharing of each others' physical, spiritual, intellectual, and emotional gifts.
- *Companionship*. The togetherness of experiencing a life shared in common through the years, and having a caring person by your side during those inevitable lonely moments of life.
- *Problem-solving*. Having the benefit of a trustworthy person's knowledge and wisdom in tackling life's problems.
- *Procreating*. Together creating, nurturing, and educating

children. To do this is to have a share in shaping the successive generations of people who inhabit the earth.

● *Unifying.* To create harmony between two people. When two individuals are drawn to each other, and held together, by the force of attraction, the result is a new creation possessing the features of the two as well as attributes of the combination. The unity between a man and a woman is the building block of a unified humanity. The couple serves as the connecting bond that links them with their children, parents, relatives, neighbors, and friends. This circle of unity, begun by the marriage of two individuals, has the potential to expand and include the whole world. Without unity at this fundamental level, the high ideals of a united humanity are not likely to be realized.

● *Greater well-being.* Most illnesses, suicide, and other miseries are higher among single people than married ones. A National Conference on Preventive Medicine in America issued a position paper stating that the incidence of illness, early death, and many other misfortunes is significantly greater among single people than those who are married.[10] Additionally, other reports[15] show that married people are healthier and, on the average, live longer than those who are unmarried.

● *Maturing.* It is in marriage that two adults who have been fairly self-contained, self-oriented, and independent evolve into a new and more mature role. They learn interdependence and sharing in a most intimate manner. The husband and wife learn to be responsive to each other's needs, expectations, likes and dislikes. The union of the two requires certain adjustments, which include giving up some personal privileges in order to benefit from their joint gifts. Each will have to make sacrifices, learn to care deeply about the other, and stand ready to share in all the consequences of the partnership. Acquisition of these qualities makes for a more mature person.

A good marriage is one of the greatest achievements in life. We must put as much, or more, effort into it as we put into our careers. A successful marriage energizes us and makes other achievements possible, but the turmoil and emotional drain of a bad marriage – or a series of bad marriages – harms other aspects of life as well.

BI-RACIAL AND INTERCULTURAL MARRIAGES

World trade, study abroad, tourism and immigration are taking greater and greater numbers of people across national boundaries. We are in close association with peoples who were – for all practical purposes – non-existent to our ancestors. The new interdependence of nations is continually bringing closer people who were previously separated.

Consequently there are more and more marriages between people of different backgrounds. This is an inevitable and beautiful result of growing global unity. Differences in skin color, culture, nationality, and religion should not be barriers; after all, humanity is one and this fundamental oneness transcends any differences. We are all far more alike biologically than most people think.[16] There are certain advantages and disadvantages in bi-racial and intercultural marriages.

- *Better genetic pool.* The farther apart a woman and man are genetically, the greater the likelihood of producing healthy children. When the genetic stock of the partners comes from widely separated ancestors, the probability that both will be carriers of the same set of defect-producing genes is greatly reduced.
- *Cultural enrichment.* The two culturally different partners will bring with them their respective tastes, perspectives, and ways of doing things that can considerably enrich the union.
- *Greater unification.* When the partners from different backgrounds marry, they become living examples of the unification of all of mankind in one human family.

There are also difficulties in mixed marriages – none of them are insurmountable, however, in our view.

- *Communication gap.* Different backgrounds may cause problems in communication. A little extra effort and sensitivity should take care of this difficulty, and the partners should take the time to study each other's background to avoid misunderstanding. By so doing, the couple can in fact create a greater harmony than is usually the case.

● *Prejudice from outsiders*. There was a time when many countries had laws forbidding marriage between people of different races. These laws have been eliminated almost everywhere in the world. Yet prejudice against people of another race, religion or ethnic background still exists in some places and it can be very strong. Couples who wish to marry in spite of this prejudice must recognize the stress that will be placed on the marriage. They will have to be prepared to withstand it, through a greater effort at making their marriage work.

● *Differences of values and tastes*. Sometimes problems arise because each partner has been accustomed to different methods of doing things, different preferences for food, and other culturally rooted matters.

Our own marriage is an intercultural one. It has lasted for over three decades and we hope that it will last to the end of time. We have been successful in resolving many of our vast cultural and personal differences. The differences challenged the marriage, but did not break it. As a result, our family has a unique subculture – a hybrid between our respective heritages, and it has brought great mutual satisfaction and enrichment.

INGREDIENTS OF A SUCCESSFUL MARRIAGE

Successful marriages have certain ingredients – some of them are listed here and discussed more fully in subsequent sections. Each partner in the marriage should have a healthy and mature understanding of these factors.

● *Self-discovery*. It is about knowing who one really is. Without developing a greater awareness of one's inner being, little growth is possible. Self-discovery makes each person aware of his or her basic uniqueness as a human being – likes, dislikes, hopes and fears.

● *Self-acceptance*. Coming to term with what one is, as well as accepting what one is evolving into – physically, spiritually, intellectually, and emotionally. Self-acceptance is not the same as resignation, which is the acceptance of mediocrity and abandonment of growth.

● *Self-love*. Deep, sincere sense of love and appreciation for oneself. This form of love is not the sick love of narcissism. It is a conviction of one's value and worth, a love that nurtures and protects. It makes possible the expenditure of one's resources for one's own care and betterment.

● *Self-reverence*. Reverence goes beyond love; it is love combined with respect. Self-reverence sets the agenda for the person's life. It determines how the person treats himself or herself, and it channels the energies toward growth.

● *Honesty*. Being what one is. Dropping the mask, stopping pretenses, getting rid of phony façades, and displaying one's true reality for inspection by oneself, and the partner. This honesty will put us to work, and will compel us to strive to become the very best that we can be.

● *Self-directedness*. To feel, speak, and act what one believes and what one values. To avoid blindly taking on the roles that others expect one to play.

● *Respect*. Both for oneself and the spouse. Respect allows love to flourish, and provides affirmation and justification for feeling close to another.

● *Compatibility*. Reduces friction, enhances enjoyment of sharing, and strengthens the common bond. It makes for better friendship[17] – the foundation of a good marriage.

● *Trustworthiness*. It is the bedrock of any relationship, the basis for sharing, confiding, and being at peace with each other.

● *Truthfulness*. Allows for candor, and eliminates the deadly poison of deception.

● *Faithfulness*. Insures the sanctity of the relationship. Protects the precious union from temporary temptations that can be extremely costly in the long run.

PART two

GETTING MARRIED

Getting married is a most important undertaking – particularly in a world that has brought people of diverse culture, race, and nationality into daily contact, making intercultural, interracial, and international marriage commonplace. The more we learn about the opportunities and the challenges of marriage, and the better we prepare ourselves, the greater are the chances of doing it right. In this section we discuss ways of preparing yourself to maximize your chances of marrying a worthy partner – and the attitudes and expectations that help you make the right choice and protect you against disappointment. We provide specifics about various compatibilities that are vital to a successful marriage – and help you look for them.

▶ 4 ◀

CHAPTER

THINKING ABOUT MARRIAGE

Early in adolescence, people start thinking about the one they will eventually fall in love with and marry. A picture begins to form in their minds of someone with all possible perfections. Good looks, wit, kindliness – the list becomes long and idealized. Yet one should spend less time day-dreaming and more time acquiring those very qualities one would like to see in a spouse. This fantasy about the perfect mate is not limited to adolescents; people working on their second and third marriages dream about finally finding that special someone.

Be realistic. If you want someone with a great sense of humor, you must develop one of your own. If you want someone who is truthful at all times, you must acquire that virtue yourself. Why should the wife or husband of your dreams settle for anything less? It is unrealistic to imagine that some glorious day you will find yourself magically provided with an ideal spouse – as much as we might wish it, life doesn't work that way. You need to develop your own set of good qualities to attract a good spouse.

● First, begin your search with yourself. Self-analysis at any age is useful; it helps to clarify what you are like and what is important to you.

You need to settle some important questions – or at least have a good idea about them – long before looking for a marriage partner. Life is a journey and a spouse is a traveling companion. You need to make sure that you have a fairly good idea of where you are heading, then you can discuss things with your potential spouse and see if he or she is going your way – or at least in the same general direction. You need to find out what sort of person you are. Are you fairly serious or happy-go-lucky? Do you love the outdoors or the inside of art galleries? Maybe neither, maybe both. Is your career an all-consuming interest? How do you like to spend your leisure time? What are your priorities? What do you want to accomplish in your life? Are you able to earn a living? Do you have an occupation? Are you acquiring one?

● You also need to ask yourself: Is your physical health in good order? Have you acquired sensible habits of proper nutrition and exercise that will ensure that you will be a healthy spouse and parent? What about your thoughts on spiritual matters? Is religion going to be your guide? What do you think about God? How do these thoughts determine the kind of person you want to be and the type of life you wish to lead? Of course you won't have all these questions completely figured out. But when you have your own life well enough in hand – so that you are basically happy and personally contented – it is then possible to multiply your happiness by marrying. You can only enhance whatever happiness you already have. You can't create it out of unhappiness. People who are emotionally immature, moody, and perpetually discontented are poor risks. They will look to their partners to make them happy – an expectation that is seldom fulfilled.

Later in Part II, we will discuss a checklist of qualities to look for in a potential marriage partner. You should also use this checklist for your own improvement, for there is no point in wishing for a partner far better than yourself. By improving your own qualities, you will not only attract a better spouse, you will become a finer person in your own right.

EXPECTATIONS ABOUT MARRIAGE

Marriage is one of the most important undertakings in life – and people rightly expect a lot from it. Some of these expectations are realistic, others are not. For a marriage to succeed, it must rest on a firm commitment: both sides must want it to work. And unrealistic expectations can seriously jeopardize the marriage.

"Both individual experience and statistical surveys make it clear that almost everyone suffers severe disappointment within a few months after marriage . . . couples married for an average of one year indicated that they felt marriage was different from what they had expected."[12] This high rate of dissatisfaction is alarming. Why is it that so many express some degree of disappointment with their marriage? Unrealistic or wrong expectations guarantee disappointment. Consider the following disgruntled comments:

> Frankly, I didn't know what I was getting into. I had funny ideas about marriage. I really thought that it would be very different from what it turned out to be. I guess, above all, it was a lot of work and not much fun. Besides, it seemed that we didn't agree on anything. The gloss of our brief courtship began to wear out during the first couple of weeks. Then, our true selves introduced themselves and what we saw, neither of us liked. So we decided to cut our losses and we split. Maybe I'll get lucky next time.

But luck has little to do with anything. In marriage – like everything else in life – the best way to insure good luck is by making your own luck. Shunning wrong attitudes and unrealistic expectations is a giant step toward good luck.

COMMON FAULTY ATTITUDES

● *I'll be in a perpetual state of bliss.* Marriage is a merging and submerging of two personalities into a common life. Even when the partners are perfectly matched, marriage will not automatically be marvelous all the time. It is simply wrong-headed to assume that it will be all fun and play. A lot of work, from interpersonal adjustment to mundane daily chores, goes into marriage.

● *I'll be loved and respected.* It all depends on how much love and respect you start with. Just as important is how hard you work, on a day-to-day basis, to keep earning love and respect.

● *I'll get my own way.* Yes, but only 50 percent of the time. The other 50 percent is your partner's share. Trouble starts when either is unwilling to accept this split down the middle.

● *I'll be taken care of.* Marriage is not a free ride. Certainly you may expect some of your needs to be taken care of, but you must also reciprocate. It is a venture of working together and benefiting together. Marriage is a two-horse carriage.

● *I'll be free.* The longing to get away from the confines of the parental home, the curfews, and the restrictions can exaggerate the attractions of marriage. The new address may prove to be just as restrictive and unfulfilling as the old one.

● *I'll have a perfect spouse.* Yes, but only if you accept him or her as is, without constant pounding to turn him or her into your idea of perfection. That's why you do all your weighing and measuring before you get married (see Chapter 7).

● *I'll never be lonely.* Loneliness and being alone are two different things. There are many married couples who are terribly lonely and some unmarried persons who are not lonely at all. It all depends on what kind of mutually loving and nurturing bond the two of you will forge together.

● My *spouse will be the solution to all my problems.* If you make your choice wisely, you should be the answer to some of each other's problems and work together or individually on the rest of them. No one person can be the total solution to anyone's problems.

● *Marriage will end my miseries.* Not so. If you have longstanding difficulties while you are single, don't expect marriage to change all that magically. Happiness must come from within the individual. No person is likely to succeed in ending another's inner discontent.

● My *spouse will satisfy all my needs.* You should meet many of your needs personally and not expect the spouse or anyone else to satisfy all of them for you. Husbands and wives are companions, nurturers, and friends – but they are not all-inclusive purveyors of all our needs and wants.

● *Love will see us through all problems.* It takes more than love to make a successful marriage. Love is not the solution to every problem. It is certainly the energizer, the comforter, and the unifier of the couple. But it must be combined with work, compromise, and even personal sacrifice to see the marriage through all problems.

● *Having children is the answer.* Many people think having children will improve an ailing marriage. They reason that the children will bring them closer to each other. Perhaps. But children can add more stress to a strained relationship.[18]

ATTRACTION AND MARRIAGE

A good marriage is like a strong chemical bond, such as that of hydrogen and oxygen making up water. The union of hydrogen and oxygen survives severe temperature changes, becoming vapor, liquid, or ice while still remaining securely bonded. An extreme force, such as intense electric current, is required to separate the two. It is from this fundamental attraction that rivers flow, oceans are formed, and life is sustained.

Similarly, strong attraction makes for a lasting marriage – while those based on minimal attraction form shaky and unstable unions that can easily fall apart in response to adversity or a stronger attraction encountered down the road. A successful marriage depends on the presence of physical, emotional, intellectual and spiritual attractions.

● *Physical attraction.* When a union is based primarily on only physical attraction, it is more likely to falter. After a while, sexual desire may taper off. Wrinkles appear under the eyes, the hairline recedes, chins double, and various other physical imperfections may come along to shatter illusions.

At the same time, other potential partners begin to look very desirable. The chase after a new physical attraction may deal a severe blow to the present bond. In some instances, there is a sense of empty urgency. A frantic effort is launched to abandon the current spouse – who is no longer physically so appealing – in favor of the new ideal before it is too late. The consequences are nearly always the same. The attractions are often superficial, the search is illusory, and the conquest itself a disappointment – as reflected by the high failure rates of second and third marriages.[19] Physical attraction, while important, should not be the sole basis of marriage.

● *Emotional attraction*. There has to be a positive emotional component to marrying someone – a feeling of excitement and love. But emotions and reason are like water and oil. Each has its place – but they don't mix all that well. Occasionally emotions and reason may be in agreement. Just as often they are not. When there is disagreement between the head and the heart, our advice is to go with the head. It's nice to be crazy about her or him – if there are no major indications that you shouldn't. If there are, just don't be crazy and say "I do".

There are all kinds of emotional traps to avoid. Some people try to find the father in the husband or the mother in the wife, for example. Other people's thinking gets foggy when they are in love. They may try to sweep away any doubts by all kinds of phony reasoning – rationalization. People in love may feel that he or she is the only one who has ever really understood them. It feels good when they are together and everything else can go away, as far as they are concerned.

● *Intellectual attraction*. A couple may be strongly drawn to each other by a meeting of minds. They find that they think alike on many issues, have similar tastes in the arts or the same interests in the sciences. Their occupations may be in the same field or fascinating to each other by being different.

There is lots for them to talk about. They seem never to get enough of each other's mind. There is a cerebral appeal between them. Obviously, this is another wonderful basis for building a lifelong relationship, as long as the other important attractions are also present. Similar intellectual interests and capacities is a definite plus. It allows the couple to enjoy each other's conversation and companionship through many thousands of hours spent together. Neither one will be forced to look for someone else to talk to.

● *Moral attraction*. Time and again we mention compatibility, because perfect compatibility means perfect harmony. And perfect harmony between a couple is the surest way of keeping them together. Incompatibility is the flip side, and can destroy a relationship. So you need compatibility of moral values between you. If you value truthfulness as the foundation of all virtues – something that should never be compromised – you certainly don't want to marry a habitual liar. If you want to devote your life, for example, to religious service, you don't want to marry an atheist. There has to be substantial agreement between the two of you on these matters to avoid constant clashes.

We personally knew a wonderful woman who endured this type of incompatibility for over 60 years. She was a devotedly religious person who wanted to attend every function of her faith. The husband, on the other hand, was a confirmed atheist who did everything he could to undermine his wife's belief and participation. He even resented her offer of compromise – going to her religious functions only occasionally.

It is the exception, rather than the rule, to find the perfect match – a person who meets all our expectations. But while we should be realistic, we should have a sense of excitement about marriage and about the very special person who is going to be the pivot of our lives. And the key to making a good marriage is self-preparation. This is the topic of the next chapter.

▶ 5 ◀

CHAPTER

GETTING YOURSELF READY

Whether you are marrying for the first, second or third time, you need to prepare yourself. Some important preparations are listed below:

- Form a positive, but realistic, attitude toward marriage. Marriage holds lots of promise, if the two of you work at making it come true. Ventures entered into with a positive attitude are more likely to succeed.
- Prepare yourself for making the required compromises and sacrifices in a give-and-take situation.
- See marriage as a partnership of two equals, devoted to the well-being of each other.
- Work hard at developing those very same qualities that you like to see in your spouse – qualities such as truthfulness, sharing, caring, kindness, fidelity, compassion, and so forth.
- Get yourself ready physically, through healthy eating and proper exercise.
- Get your finances and career matters in good order. This is a major area of contention and a leading cause of divorce in the United States and other countries.[20]

THE FEMININE CHALLENGE

Women, as a newly emancipated underclass, have to work harder to adjust to the format of the new cultural paradigm. Some of the challenges that face women are listed below.

- *Be a 'stand-alone' person.* Develop those qualities that make a complete and independent human being – so that you are valued for what you, yourself, are rather than as someone else's accessory.
- *Don't wait for someone to come along to confer status on you.* You don't have to be someone's wife to be counted. You establish your own status by your own accomplishment. There is nothing that a man can do that a woman cannot. Men have no monopoly on anything. Living out of a suitcase mentally – waiting for a man to come along and confer personhood on you – is unwise. Forge ahead with your own life plans.
- *Develop your career and interests, and set up your own household.* Enjoy life now – not at some far-off time when a man comes along to make you come alive at last. By carrying on with your life as a whole person, you also enhance your chances for meeting an equally mature man to marry. You will not have wasted years waiting around.
- *Don't be a helpless female.* Well-adjusted men realize that a strong woman – developed emotionally and intellectually – is preferable as a lifelong partner to a helpless and immature female. Marriage is a partnership. Be a partner with great assets. You will be valued, cherished, and loved for it.
- *Don't be vengeful.* The new marriage paradigm is based on fairness, love, and a sense of justice. Don't abuse your newly earned privileges by being vengeful – holding men responsible for historical inequities. Just look ahead and build on the new foundation.

ATTRACTING A MATE

The matchmaker is a figure of the past, and parents and relatives play minor roles in bringing marriageable people together, while friends and acquaintances are sometimes helpful. In the age of emancipation, the woman or the man must take the initiative and they are the ones who are primarily responsible for finding their own life partner.

But how does one go about attracting a mate? By relying on common sense? Common sense is not always as sensible as it sounds; it is often plain contradictory. When it comes to love, relationships, and attractions, which commonsense saying should be our guide? We face many contradictions, such as, "Opposites attract" versus "Birds of a feather flock together"; or "Absence makes the heart grow fonder," versus "Out of sight, out of mind."

The best thing to do is to go with known facts. Research has substantiated the importance of several factors in attracting a member of the opposite sex.

● *Proximity*. Somewhat related to the commonsense saying of "Out of sight, out of mind" is the notion of proximity – nearness in physical space. It plays a pivotal role in making friends and forming relationships. Why is proximity important? It provides the opportunity for people to interact. People are more available to each other, and availability is a powerful influence. So go ahead and actively look for the spouse of your dreams. Cast a broad net, and don't arbitrarily exclude any possibilities. This is not decision time, only looking time. Go to places and get involved in activities that are likely to attract your type. Join clubs, religious groups, volunteer organizations. Once you see a possibility, you may want to follow the advice of David Givens,[21] a research anthropologist who has studied courtship behavior of people in airports, cafeterias, parks, parties, and other settings. The work of Givens and others shows the importance of other factors, in addition to proximity, in attracting a mate.

● *Attractiveness*. Aristotle observed that "Beauty is a greater recommendation than any letter of introduction." Humans value beauty so much that they tend to equate it with 'good'.[22] In other words, we do judge a book by its cover. We tend to believe that attractive people are more likely to find good jobs – and they do; more likely to marry well and lead a fuller, happier life. Physical appearance is profoundly important in many spheres of life. In attracting a mate, it can be the difference between finding a good one or a bad one – or even none at all. You may say that this is something you can't help; that you are not attractive. This is an excuse, and a poor one at that. Everyone can become more attractive by adopting a sensible diet and adhering to a program of personal hygiene and exercise. We need to work with and develop our different potentials. Even those who seem to be naturally gorgeous must work hard at maintaining it, and attractiveness is something that lends itself to development more than many other attributes.

● *Similarity*. The greater the similarity between the personal characteristics, attitudes and beliefs of two people, the greater their attraction to each other. Homogamy – the tendency of like to marry like – has been substantiated by hundreds of studies investigating characteristics such as age, race, nationality, religion, social status, education, previous marital history, intelligence, emotional and psychological attributes, physical health, social attitudes, and even height. The verdict is nearly unanimous – like tends to marry like. Having similar social attitudes seems to be a more important factor in attraction than the sharing of personal characteristics. To make it easy on yourself and to enhance your chances for connecting with a future mate, you should concentrate on people who share your social attitudes. This allows the two of you to build a relationship of reassurance and approval, a vital start for a possible marriage and an indispensable requisite for a lifelong journey of togetherness.

● *Complementarity*. We have just emphasized the importance of similarity, and now we are going to tell you that the differences between two people can be equally important attractants. This is the case when different personality traits create a sense of completeness between the couple when they are joined together – each provides what the other lacks. Early work by Robert Winch[23] demonstrated the fact that people tend to be attracted to a potential mate who holds the greatest promise of meeting their needs. Subsequent work in this area upholds the importance of the general notion of complementarity. Complementarity in the sense of role compatibility is pivotal. That is, if one partner has a large need to dominate, he or she is more likely to be attracted to a deferential person than to another dominating personality. If a person is socially reticent, retiring, and non-assertive, he or she may find qualities of gregariousness and assertiveness desirable characteristics in a mate. It is, therefore, wise to seek out individuals who seem to complement your personality and social characteristics. By so doing you are likely to enhance your chances for not only attracting a mate, but also forming a satisfying marriage.

- *Appearance*. Present yourself in ways that tell others whether you are or you are not interested. Your personal appearance, such as clothes and hair-style, can say "notice me," or "skip me." Appearance is of great importance in what is called the group's erotic-popularity hierarchy, which operates in all social settings. Individuals are placed at various levels of the hierarchy, through a complicated set of procedures. In many instances each individual is discussed by the group or its subset – in his or her absence – and a consensus is reached about that person's erotic quotient. Is she a ten, a zero, or somewhere in between? And considerable pressure – often latent – is applied to individuals to bond within their assigned erotic quotient. Hence, you need to pay attention to your appearance. This attention to appearance becomes even more important when you are entering a new social grouping – such as a social club, a service order, or a new workplace.
- *Approachability*. Show your approachability to the person by gazing a little longer when looking without making eye contact. You can smile and if there is interest on the other's part, strike up a conversation. What you say is not particularly important. Just say something. You don't have to wait for the man to make the move. If you do, it may end up as a lost opportunity. In the new paradigm, women are equally entitled to initiate friendship with men. Of course women have to be a bit discreet as well as smart in so doing. You need to use good judgment and taste. But practice the art at home. Better yet, with a trusting friend or family member. Go through the

motions. By so doing you become better at it and you lose the unwarranted inhibitions that might let the opportunity slip by. Men, as well as women, find it flattering when a member of the opposite sex shows interest in them. That in itself can be a spark for starting a valuable relationship.

- *Interaction*. Once you are past the first obstacle – having started a conversation with the person – some experts such as Givens suggest that a man should speak slowly, tilt his head to one side, and nod while the woman speaks. A woman should turn toward the man, and relax her shoulders. These gestures and bodily orientations make for a friendly atmosphere that facilitates attraction. Obviously, human courtship is not a genetically programmed, stereotyped routine. Yet there are activities that facilitate the process as well as those that can abort it. It is always a good practice to show consideration and care without projecting the image of a 'lamb.' People value challenging and exciting partners, as long as there is a fundamental sense of agreement and sharing.

The above suggestions do not exhaust the possible strategies. Yet, if you follow them, you are likely to enhance your chances for attracting a mate.

TWELVE PILLARS OF A GOOD MARRIAGE

Building a good marriage requires know-how, some tools, and motivation. This book is devoted to these essential ingredients. At this point, we would like to describe what we consider to be the twelve pillars of a good marriage.

- *Attraction and love*. It is attraction and love that brings two people together and keeps them together. You can't live on love, but you can't have a good marriage without it either. Like any living thing, love can grow and flourish, but it can also wither and die. The best indication of a good marriage is when love keeps on growing – when the bond between the pair gets even more precious with each passing day.
- *Respect*. In a good marriage, respect permeates the relationship. This doesn't mean that the two are cautious or

formal in their interaction. It simply reflects – in things that they do and say – that they genuinely respect each other. Where there is respect, love can thrive. But where there is no respect – or worse yet, where there is contempt – love can hardly survive.

● *Compatibility*. A good marriage is about two people heading in the same direction – and at the same time – together. Without an overall compatibility of life goals and personal preferences, the union will be tested at every step. It is hard to imagine any two people being perfectly compatible, but we are not talking about a hypothetical world of perfection. We are talking about having a good marriage. And to have a good marriage, it is wise to start with as much compatibility as possible. Then, keep working to increase compatibility without forcing your partner to make all the necessary adjustments.

● *Commitment*. Commitment is the cord that connects a couple. It must be strong to begin with and must be constantly reinforced. A universal force of nature aims at separation, decomposition, and reduction of all complex systems to their simplest components. Marriage is no exception. All kinds of personal and social forces aim at the breakup of the union, the minute it is formed. A good marriage demands unconditional commitment on the part of the partners to resist the powerful and varied forces that aim to end their togetherness. A couple we know – married happily for over 40 years – confided that, in their marriage, commitment was the single most important factor in keeping them together. They successfully fought back the numerous serious blows that aimed to break up their union. They said proudly, "Now, only death can part us. But, even then, we'll be together in the next worlds of God." Now that is a good marriage. Forty years and counting and looking forward to spending eternity together.

● *Compassion and care*. Life is wonderful. But it is also a war of unceasing battles. Battling work demands, those of child-bearing and child-raising, health problems, financial hardships, and personal tragedies strike the couple as a pair as well as individually. Hence the need for unconditional compassion and care. A marriage that provides those things is a haven of comfort. In this impersonal age, the need for intimate compassion and care is even greater within marriage. Each partner must be prepared to share not only in the joys, but also the sorrows – big and small – of the other.

The story of a couple we know demonstrates the kind of compassion and care that we are talking about. He is 77 years old, she is 73. Up to five years ago, both the man and the woman were in excellent shape – outstanding individuals of numerous interests and activities. Then tragedy struck in a freak accident. The wife slipped, while walking, and a brain concussion confined her to a wheelchair, with additional complications. The vivacious, active, and outstanding human being we knew was suddenly transformed into an incapacitated person. How is the husband dealing with this tragedy? He is a paragon of compassion and care. He still works at his job – only half-days. He wheels his beloved wife around to many of the old functions that were dear to her heart. Frail as he is, he lifts her 50 lb wheelchair in and out of the car, up and down the stairs. He stays up nights to assist her with her frequent needs. He takes short naps in the afternoons. Above all, he does all this with sincere love and without the slightest complaint. She would have done the same for him, we are sure.

● *Preparation*. Marriage is a life journey that we take in the company of a special person. The best journeys are those that are well thought out; the ones that we fully prepare ourselves for; the ones for which we anticipate the requirements. If you go on an African safari, for example, you need certain inoculations; you need to learn something about the place; and you need proper provisions for it. Being unprepared is not the same as being spontaneous – it is more often a reflection of impulsiveness or laziness. Preparation is a key to a good marriage. We must prepare ourselves to compromise, to be ready to share, to give up some personal freedom, to accept responsibility, and to work hard.

● *Competence*. Competence is closely related to preparation. A good marriage requires two competent partners – each capable of functioning as 'stand-alone' individuals. It is a risky thing to enter marriage in the hope that your partner will have enough competence for both of you. You can have different degrees and types of competencies that, when pooled together, make for synergy. That is the secret of a good partnership. Think of marriage preparation as setting out a banquet. You have your very own 'table' with different 'dishes' (qualities and competencies). When two people get married, it is like pushing their previously separate tables together and sharing their meal. Is your table reasonably full to begin with? Or do you expect the other person to bring a full table? Are you capable of going through life – if you have to – without someone else taking care of you? Do you have the minimum life skills necessary in the complicated modern age, with all its varied technological and social demands? If the answer is affirmative, then you are an asset to your mate. If not, you need to get on with it and acquire the needed competencies – such as a profession that can provide you with means of livelihood, and skills to handle the varied demands of an independent life. Even after marriage, you should continue honing these skills. You must be prepared to take over if temporary or permanent incapacities afflict your spouse.

● *Communication*. Silence is not always golden. Neither is being a chatterbox a virtue. But sensible and effective communication is both golden and virtuous. A marriage that does not communicate is, at best, stalled. More likely, it is not a good one and on its way to breaking up at the opportune moment. The old cliché, "My wife (or husband) doesn't understand me" may be a ruse for exploiting a member of the opposite sex, but equally often it does represent a measure of the truth. The couple may talk, but they don't get through to each other. You need to get into the habit of effectively communicating all your concerns with the closest human being in your life – immediately. Don't wait till the marriage gets on an even keel, till it is strong, till you get to know each other better. It is candid and caring communication that makes all those things happen, not the other way around.

● *Consultation*. One-sided decisions and actions, perhaps more than anything else, work against a good marriage. They often end it altogether. Talk it over with your partner, before making decisions or taking actions that affect both your lives. Remember that he or she is a full partner in this most vital business. Obviously, you shouldn't overdo it and carry consultation into the realm of absurdity; you will also want to do a great many things without letting each other know – like beautiful little surprises that add spice to life. You should hardly consult with her on whether or not she would like flowers from you on her birthday, or with him about arranging a candle-lit dinner at home.

● *Compromise*. An indispensable tool of a good marriage is compromise. The willingness to bend, to adjust, and to make allowances for the other's preferences makes marriage an exercise in togetherness and maturity. Compromise is not the same as giving in or surrendering to the other person. One-sided 'niceness' is no more part of a good marriage than is one-sided decision-making. Healthy compromise involves making some personal adjustments – and some sacrifices – for the benefit of the marriage. Talking of compromise reminds us of the story of a newly wed young couple we know. In the course of conversation, we said something about the importance of compromise in marriage. The young, starry-eyed husband, an immensely affable bear of a man, responded, "Our marriage has gone beyond compromise. We vie with each other to let the other person have their way." It sounded like the voice of early honeymoon – which it was – speaking. We haven't met very many people who are as mature and happy as our dear young friends. We still believe in the merits and the need for compromise.

● *Work*. Marriage is work. And we know of no work that is devoid of rewards, and of no reward worthy of the term that is not earned through work. We are convinced that working for the marriage – unlike many other investments in life – is a sure way of reaping the rewards of our efforts. Much of the work that goes into keeping a marriage vibrant and healthy is simple drudgery – where household chores often head the list; some of the work is tolerable; and some might even be pleasant. Yet it is still work. And there are ways of making even the most unpleasant chores less arduous. We have some pointers on this, and you can think of your own ingenious approaches to the task.

● *Expectations*. Realistic expectations in marriage are like optimal ballast in a ship. Without them a marriage capsizes as surely as a ship. You need to enter marriage with optimism, a sense of excitement, and the belief that it is going to be an improvement over your present single state. Otherwise, why do it? But having unreasonably high expectations from marriage or the spouse is a sure recipe for disappointment. A good marriage makes allowances for both partners being human. They are neither perfect nor are they likely to be perfectible. And marriage itself – being a human activity of two less than perfect beings – is not likely to be a perfect haven of all good. But perfection is something that we strive for. If we succeed in even approximating it, we have done well indeed.

Now that we have some ideas about the ingredients of a good marriage, we are ready to go to work.

▶ 6 ◀

CHAPTER

FINDING & CHOOSING A SPOUSE

Everyone looks for a perfect match in marriage. But a perfect match is not one's clone; even if you found your clone, the marriage would likely be very boring. A perfect match is not sameness, but the harmony of differences between two people. Blending of differences can be very exciting and enriching to marriage. It makes for the spirit of what Scott Peck calls 'community.'[24] Marriage is the smallest and yet the most fundamental community.

A successful marriage is a harmonious paradox – a harmony of differences. It is a paradox because two very different individuals manage to find harmony between them, like a violin and a piano – two quite different instruments making music that neither can produce alone. This shared harmony in marriage is not achieved through long battles of will to force the partner to become more and more like oneself. It is produced by the force of synergy and complementarity, where differences enrich the union.

Certain musical instruments – as different as they are from each other – are highly compatible. Other instruments, each beautiful in its own right, don't harmonize together. Finding a spouse is also about two people making beautiful music together instead of nerve-shattering noise. This section is intended to help you find the compatible music-maker of your life.

Please keep in mind:

- We are not saying that you should choose only a partner who meets all the qualifications listed in this section.
- We know that most people do not have a long list of highly qualified candidates to choose from.
- We only want you to consider what you might want to look for in a spouse and help you attract that person.
- You will have to make the final judgment – whether or not a person, on balance, is someone you wish to marry.

DATING AND COURTSHIP

Dating and courtship vary greatly from place to place. In some societies – mostly in the East – many marriages are arranged by the parents or other intermediaries. In western countries, the individual takes the initiative by dating. But western-style dating is not always the best way of choosing a spouse.[12] The qualities one looks for in a good date may be very different from what one wants in a spouse. A person may date someone with high social status or physical attractiveness to impress friends – using the date to publicize one's own desirability to others, instead of being genuinely attached. Dating can be a way of assuring oneself that one is desirable to others, or signaling one's worth, or simply having fun in social activities.

Each human being has numerous facets. So there is no 'real me' – instead, there are many shades of the same general theme. Courtship is the time to find out about the many faces of your future partner – not just the Saturday-night face. Don't become fixated on one of the faces that is particularly alluring to you, because sooner or later the others will introduce themselves. The unpleasant faces are seldom discovered by cursory inspections, because we usually put on the best face for public display.

Dating may start many years before young people can actually marry and settle down. In some places, one may begin dating at twelve years of age and marry as long as a decade or more later. Having a boyfriend or girlfriend becomes a way of life. Knowing that another partner can easily be found, young people are quite accustomed to breaking up whenever a relationship runs into difficulty. This easy in, easy out dating may become a habit that one carries into marriage. Here are some points to consider about dating:

- *Marrying out of tiring.* Forming and breaking relationships is exhausting, and eventually, you may just go ahead and marry your latest date without really having had a chance to look at the person as a prospective lifelong partner.
- *Not getting what you have seen.* In our view, western-style dating, with all its privileges and irresponsibilities, is not a good way of finding a suitable spouse. The two individuals often meet each other when they are at their artificial best – all rested, prettied up, ready and eager to have a good time in the seductive aura of the special occasion. No one can be expected to keep a cool head in examining the potential partner's true personality and character in the highly artificial – and often sexually-charged – setting of a Saturday night date. The man and the woman may say and do things that will impress each other, often masking their true selves in order to continue the relationship. This pretense quickly ends and you may be shocked by the real person you have married.
- *Preparing when very young.* Very young people should enjoy the fun and companionship of their friends in groups without pairing off. When freed from the pressures and stressful competition of dating, they can then spend their energies on more fully developing themselves intellectually and emotionally.
- *Evaluating yourself.* Before even beginning to look for a marriage partner, you should develop a good insight about yourself – your likes, priorities, and goals in life.
- *Where to look.* This depends on what kind of person you are looking for. Courtship should be carried out in settings that closely resemble daily life itself. Settings such as the workplace, schools, sports and other clubs, meetings of organizations, religious gatherings, and the like, should provide a true testing ground for a preliminary assessment.

It is in the arena of normal daily life that one's true character can be revealed and realistically observed. It is here that the woman can ascertain for herself whether or not she would want to consider him to be her permanent companion, the father of her children, and her most intimate friend. It is here that the man can perform a similar assessment of a potential wife.

Of course we are not implying that the couple should never have any time together alone. But we are emphasizing the importance of initially studying and getting to know each other in normal settings.

● *A closer look.* Once you find a possible candidate, you need to take a closer look – talking about life goals, ambitions, views on children and child-raising, common likes and dislikes, without necessarily being in intimate settings where physical attraction can dominate the situation. Long walks together are ideal for these kinds of discussions.

Why is all this talk necessary? The rate of change and the complexity of life in this century have made people themselves highly complex. In the past, the common cultural assumptions of traditional masculine and feminine roles made things far easier. Within each culture, 'the husband' was supposed to do this, 'the wife' to do that. Learning from their parents and neighbors as role models, each partner generally knew what to do as well as what to expect of the other. Selection was largely a matter of personality and physical attraction and was often simplified by the fact that each person knew only a limited number of people.

Today, nearly every marriage is, in a sense, cross-cultural – even if the couple grew up across the street from each other. People of different ethnic, racial and religious backgrounds are increasingly coming together, but in addition lifestyles within cultures have multiplied at a dizzying rate through exposure to higher levels of education, travel, books, movies, television, and so on – each with its own influences on ways of thinking. It is essential, therefore, that the couple spend a lot of time talking together and exploring a multitude of subjects. There is a wise American Indian proverb, "Don't judge any person until you have walked two moons in their moccasins."

MAKING AN IMPRESSION

After you initially meet someone who seems promising, you naturally want to make a good impression to continue the relationship. Making the first impression is extremely important, because people tend to paint an elaborate picture of others on the basis of first impressions. When we see one trait in someone, we assume that he or she has other qualities consistent with the first. This is called the halo effect. For instance, if we think someone is good-looking, we also assume that he is smart, cheerful, nice, and so forth. The halo effect plays a large role when we fall in love – in those early stages when we really don't know the person but attribute a lot of good qualities to him because we like him. This halo effect is the main reason for the importance of first impressions. You need to make the first impression a very good one. If you succeed, the person you are trying to impress will attribute a lot of good things to you. They make an emotional investment in you and thereafter do what they can to protect it. They even fiercely resist contradictory information and facts. Then the rest is up to you – either confirming the first impression by further niceness or eroding it by displaying negative qualities that will eventually wipe out the positive early impression.

PHYSICAL APPEARANCE

Physical appearance plays a profound role in people's lives – the friendship and companionship of attractive people is preferred over that of unattractive people.[25] And personal grooming, diet, and exercise do wonders for our appearance. You definitely need to look good to stay attractive to your spouse. Marriage – and having found a mate – should not be taken as a license for sloppiness and self-neglect. If you don't care enough for your own appearance, why should anyone else care for you? A known fact is that we end up marrying people of equal attractiveness to our own.[26] Implication: if you want an attractive spouse, make yourself as attractive as you can.

▸ 7 ◂

CHAPTER

SPOUSE EVALUATION

When you are considering sharing a lifetime with someone, you had better do a little checking. Go beyond superficial appearances and check things out; then make up your mind. You can always decide to ignore all the counter-indications and plunge into marriage anyway. Then you'll have the satisfaction of having made a mistake knowingly!

A wise young friend who was considering marriage once told us, "I know that all marriages need hard work to succeed, no matter who the partners are. What I want to find is someone who is worth all the work we will have to do together."

There are all kinds of things that you need to know about a prospective spouse – such as sense of humor, life values, goals, ambitions, artistic inclinations, and so forth. What if it turns out that she loves to play the drums? Playing the drums is her passion. Can you put up with a lifetime of listening to the daily beat, or are you going to try to cure her of it? Ideally, you should do all you can to make her enjoy playing the drums more than ever.

The watchword in marriage is compromise. But this does not mean that the life you had before marriage should die and a totally new one start. There are many areas that marriage must support and nurture. Marrying should not mean abandonment of one's numerous interests, activities, and legitimate pleasures. Ideal marriages require the minimum of dislocations and adjustments. This is precisely what courtship time should be devoted to – discovering and building upon the likes, values and interests that the partners have in common.

SPOUSE SELECTION AND MATCHING

To give marriage a good start, you need to do two things. First, determine your partner's personal qualities. Second, and equally important, see if there is a good enough match between the two of you. And it is never too early or too late (whether it is your first, second, third, or fourth marriage that you are contemplating) for you to start developing your own qualities so that you will have the same desirable characteristics that you seek in a mate. Further, start making goals for yourself long before you are actually ready to get married – even in early adolescence. Remember that studies show that likes attract likes, confirming what we are told in Aesop's Fables, "There can be little liking where there is no likeness." So, if you want a partner with certain qualifications, you had better start acquiring them yourself. For best selection and matching, four areas should be considered: moral values and attributes; artistic, affectional and intellectual attributes; physical attributes; and interests, habits and life goals.

MORAL VALUES AND ATTRIBUTES

This category deals with one's moral character. No human being is a paragon of virtue, but you want your special someone to have an abundance of moral and ethical qualities, and these qualities are not for the benefit of some abstract doctrine rooted in obsolete religious thinking. They are indispensable to any relationship and critical to marriage. Without them, the entire fabric of human existence unravels. Hence, you need to do a bit of work in assessing your future partner.

Does he or she have high ethical standards and believe in the sanctity of life and the equality of men and women? Is he or she compassionate toward people, as well as animals; tolerant towards all races, religions and ethnic backgrounds; does he or she believe in non-violence and peace; care for the environment? What about other characteristics such as truthfulness, honesty, courtesy, dependability, fairness, forgiveness, loyalty, sincerity, trustworthiness, humility, kindness, sympathy, unselfishness, courage, patience? It seems like a long list. But it is only a partial one and you can think of other qualities that can be added to it. It takes a great deal to make a human being and a great deal more to make a worthy one.

ARTISTIC, AFFECTIONAL AND INTELLECTUAL ATTRIBUTES

You also need to know about attributes that fall into this category. Is he or she open-minded, intelligent, knowledgeable, wise, mature, insightful, creative, resourceful, orderly, articulate? What about mood and disposition? Is he or she cheerful, optimistic, happy, enthusiastic, friendly, vivacious, personable, calm, supportive, easygoing? It may be important to you that he or she is poetic, artistic, musical, or literary-minded; in any case, a good sense of humor seems essential. What about qualities such as reasonableness, conscientiousness, self-discipline, self-confidence, flexibility, independence, and maturity?

PHYSICAL ATTRIBUTES

Equally important are a person's physical qualities. Is he or she healthy, strong, energetic, neat and clean? Do his or her looks appeal to you; make your heart skip a beat once in a while; make you want to cuddle, hold hands, and embrace? We can hardly give you a comprehensive list of universally desirable physical qualities, because this is primarily the realm of the heart and each heart beats to a rhythm of its own. That's why it is said that "Beauty is in the eye of the beholder." What makes for physical appeal has some universal elements, but many that are unique for each person.

INTERESTS, HABITS AND LIFE GOALS

You will want to know about your areas of agreement and disagreement in advance. The more you know about each other, the more likely it is that you will make a wise decision. There are so many things that go into making a good union or a bad one, and there has to be a great deal of compatibility to start with – at least, the compatibilities should outweigh the incompatibilities. For example, if the person you want to marry is extremely gregarious and you prefer solitude, you have an incompatibility that you should consider. But if both of you love to travel, you should know that too.

You need to discuss all kinds of matters. Do you have the same or compatible life goals? Do you agree on having children, how many, and when? What kind of commitment does each of you have to your respective career, your humanitarian or religious work? What are your hobbies; how do you feel about sports, as both spectator and participant; are concerts, ballet and theater the centerpiece of your life? What about the day-to-day matters of food and domestic lifestyle; a preference for rural, suburban or urban living; and having pets? Do you have a meeting of minds on vacations, travel, and socializing? What about your individual obligations, if any, toward parents, relatives and friends?

Are there some 'non-negotiable' aspects to life for one of you, or well-entrenched habits that the other doesn't know about? For instance, is he or she of the early-to-bed and early-to-rise type, while your day ends at midnight and begins at noon? Would this pose a big problem? It may be a blessing in disguise – you won't see enough of each other to have arguments! What about your ideas of entertainment? Is she a fanatical outdoor person who loves to spend all her leisure time playing golf, fishing, mountain-climbing and exploring the wilderness? Do you, on the other hand, prefer to do your fishing only at restaurants; are you the classic couch potato who likes to read, watch television, and be within easy commuting distance of the refrigerator?

Perhaps the most important issue to discuss is your views on finances. It is said that we live in a material world and a material world requires material means. Do you have a shared view on this and all its varied implications?

It is important that you take the time to discuss these issues – particularly those areas that might present serious problems to the marriage, as the honeymoon period gives way to reality. A good match has enough going for it to transform initial attraction into a lifetime of priceless togetherness.

▶ 8 ◀

CHAPTER

LEARNING MORE ABOUT YOUR PARTNER

Each of us will have expectations and preconceived ideas about marriage and the family – there is no way that we can avoid having them because we are raised with certain assumptions about such relationships and they become a part of us. The difficulty arises when these assumptions and expectations are not openly discussed. If these notions are not brought out and considered jointly, they may prove to be a hidden source of many misunderstandings in the future. So do more than superficial exploration of the personality you want to love and cherish for life. Discuss as many issues as you can think of. Chances are that you will never find perfect harmony, but you can certainly go a long way toward avoiding unpleasant surprises later.

For example, before getting married, the couple may want to talk about their home life as children and the kind of communication that went on within each family. How did the parents express affection and anger between themselves and to the children? Was there harmony or acrimony between the mother and father? What was discipline like? Who was the power center? How did the parents resolve conflict, cooperatively or through dominance and submission? Did the parents share interests, or did each go a separate way during leisure time? Were holiday celebrations of little or much importance? All of these aspects of the parental home will influence people's attitudes and actions when they establish their own homes.

● *Don't be afraid of disagreement.* It would be surprising if two people's expectations of how men and women should behave meshed completely. Just being aware of the expectations and assumptions imprinted on us from our childhood will make marital adjustment easier. There will be fewer surprises and less guessing at the reasons for particular behavior.

If possible, the couple should spend time with each other's parents and siblings to observe their interaction and lifestyle. This will increase an understanding of where they're coming from in a most literal sense. Unfortunately, many people do not live near their families and couples may not be able to become acquainted with each other's home life. This is all the more reason for them to take the time to talk these things over.

● *Look for the big items.* Some issues are critical. For example, let's suppose that the fellow you like doesn't believe in the equality of men and women. Obviously, you want to know whether or not he is just teasing when he makes negative comments about women. If not, is he likely to be receptive to a quick education, or is he settled in his opinion? Would you want to marry this type of man? What are the implications of his views for your goals and ambitions in life? Will you be 'allowed' to do much of anything beside household chores?

● *Protection against surprises.* Another advantage of discussing things before marriage is to protect you, to some extent, against later disappointments and surprises. For instance, by evaluating each other's character ahead of time, you are less likely to discover all sorts of flaws only two days into the honeymoon.

What happens if you find someone you're crazy about, who is a marvelous dancer, but that's about all? Of course, you could go ahead and marry him anyway, even if you know that he has numerous faults and that the two of you agree on virtually nothing. We advise against it. We feel that marriage is for keeps. It is forever. So make every effort to do it right. Look for someone who already has a sound character and shares your interests, as well as makes your heart beat a little faster. You certainly want to be attracted to him or her by your head as well as your heart.

● *Look for a true partner.* In choosing a spouse, avoid the spongy personality – the type who knows only taking and little or no giving. Someone once said that getting into marriage with all kinds of false expectations is like two people going to a picnic empty-handed – each expecting the other to bring all the food. Benjamin Franklin advised: "Keep your eyes wide open before marriage and half-closed after marriage." The idea is that you should be very careful investigating your future spouse, but after you make your choice you should be forgiving of faults, flaws, and shortcomings in each other.

FINANCIAL COMPATIBILITY

Financial difficulties and disagreements are a major cause of divorce. So spend some time during courtship doing a little preventive work. You should see if you have a meeting of minds on this issue. For instance, what if the husband had always wanted great wealth while the wife believed that they should earn only enough money to meet their basic needs, and they never discussed this before they got married?

There are so many things you need to know about your partner. Here are some that relate to the general matter of money, the value placed on material possessions, and personal habits and practices in this regard. The Rosenbaums have a useful book on this subject.[27] Some of their ideas are included here. Find out what your partner is like.

● Is he or she from a vastly different economic class?

● Would your potential spouse subscribe to a financial or business magazine and read it from cover to cover?

● Is the stock market a constant topic of interest – keeping track of interest and dividend earnings or profit and loss ratios of companies?

- Does he or she like to spend a lot of time window-shopping, bargain hunting, and simply acquiring things?
- Is your partner a rummage, garage, and yard sales addict, spending free time – week-ends and holidays – running from sale to sale?
- Must he or she buy things to feel good, being preoccupied with gifts and presents?
- Does he or she use money to manipulate, influence, or control others?
- Is money considered the sole measure of success and self-worth?
- Does your partner know how to handle and manage money?
- Is he or she a spendthrift, a risk-taker with money? Or a skinflint who hates to part with even a penny?
- Does he or she buy on credit and get into a deep hole of credit debt?
- Are expensive gifts for birthdays, anniversaries and so forth imperative?
- Is he or she someone who likes to be in sole control of the finances?

Discuss these matters and see if you have enough agreement. Can you work out compromises? Maybe your partner is very firm about certain financial ideas. Can you put up with them?

CONSIDERING CHILDREN

Having children, unavoidable and necessary in the past, is both avoidable and a luxury now. In the new paradigm children have become important because:

- *The mother has become important.* Children were always seen as a sort of appendage to the mother. Women are now increasingly valued, and hence the worth of the children they bear has risen as well.
- *Fathers are more involved with children.* More and more fathers share child-raising duties with mothers and this involvement increases appreciation for children.

● *Children are wanted.* There is the element of choice. Many parents make a conscious decision to have children, and few are burdened by an unwanted child.

● *Increased consciousness.* Human beings in general, irrespective of gender, race, nationality, religion, age, and so on, are valued as precious. Children are costly, emotionally as well as financially. They also require a great deal of time – something that modern couples find themselves increasingly short of. Of course there are potential compensations as well, but the costs are certain while the rewards may never materialize or be minimal.

Some things to keep in mind about having children:

● *Having children is a joint venture.* It is a joint venture because it requires both parents' – not only the mother's – contributions to child-raising. Also, having children demands significant changes in the life of the couple. The term 'fathering' has a broader meaning under the new paradigm. It refers to a committed and long-term role in child-raising – not just the biological function in conception. The two of you need to prepare yourselves for a joint venture of child-raising that will occupy a portion of your life for as long as you live. Even after they become adults and have children of their own, you still remain heavily invested in them and their welfare.

● *Having children is expensive.* Children require a great deal of time and emotional and financial support. Human offspring are slow to become self-sufficient and independently competent – particularly in this increasingly complex world. The technological society of today and that of the future has little use for uneducated, unskilled people. It is very harsh on those who do not acquire the educational, emotional, and spiritual tools for dealing with life. It is in the home that children start their acquisition of these tools and the parents are the on-the-spot teachers and providers.

● *Children are not ourselves reincarnated.* Love of children, in their own right, is a powerful motivation for having them.

Yet a poorly appreciated but pervasive reason in many cases is the desire of the parents to relive their own childhood vicariously through their children. Nearly all parents, often without being aware of it, practice some elements of this tendency. In some instances, this practice is mild, harmless, or even good for the child. For instance, a mother who feels that her parents did not encourage her to go to college may tend to work hard at enabling her daughter to get a college education. But the practice can also be destructive in other instances. Consider a father who feels that as a child he was the most well-behaved boy who never quarreled with anyone, always did what anyone told him, and often found people took advantage of his submissiveness. Now, as an adult, he resents his 'timid' childhood and encourages his son to be excessively assertive, fight for his rights, and not take any nonsense from anyone. The result maybe a violent social misfit – a child condemned to enacting roles that the father wanted to play himself. Or a case of a parent who was raised in a poor family. He or she seldom got much in the way of material things and entertainment. Now, the parent is showering all kinds of things and experiences on the child – trying to make up, through the child, for her or his perceived deprivations.

● *Having children is not all fun.* Romanticizing about children can lead to disillusionment when one comes face to face with reality. There will be sleepless nights to contend with after a long day's work either in the home or outside it. There are always risks of congenital or acquired illnesses – some serious and incapacitating. There are the adolescent years, which seem interminable to many unprepared parents. And the list goes on. Sounds as if we are against having children? Not at all. We had two ourselves. Two wonderful human beings who accepted the few good pieces of advice that we gave them and forgave us our many shortcomings. We are for making decisions intelligently – decisions that would enhance your well-being and minimize pain and suffering. For in-depth discussion of child-raising requirements and practices see our book, *Creating a Successful Family*.[28]

LOVE AND FANTASY

When we don't like something, we react against it. If it is an uncomfortable chair, we change the chair. If it is a disturbing thought, we do things to get rid of it or even make it pleasant – often by using fantasy, mental manipulation, and even self-deception. Sometimes, the manipulation is so skillfully done that we succeed in fooling even ourselves. We are engaged in this kind of manipulation nearly all the time, and often without being fully aware of it. What is called reality is often another form of make-believe.

The ability to manipulate the psyche is a mixed blessing. On the one hand, it can transform the most bitter of experiences into tolerable or even delectable ones. On the other hand, it can insulate us from objectivity, create false expectations, and set us up for disappointments. Falling in love with your own fantasies, projected onto someone else, is dangerous – it won't take long before you meet the real person. The result is shattered illusions and disappointment. Our advice is to keep a level head about your potential partner, and do your best to keep fantasy out of the selection process. That is the way to enhance your chances for getting what you thought you would.

THINGS TO KEEP IN MIND

In choosing a marriage partner, keep these thoughts in mind:

- You should find your future partner physically appealing to you. When you are with your special someone, your heart should pound with excitement, a warmth should run through your veins, and desire surge.
- You need compatibility of emotions, moral values, goals in life, intellect, financial concerns, and hobbies. Compatibility is the glue of the relationship.
- You must have genuine respect for each other. Without respect, there is no equality. And without equality, the relationship is in jeopardy.
- It is difficult to recommend selfishness. Yet we advise the reader to look after his or her own best interests in

selecting the most suitable marriage partner – get yourself ready and diligently examine the choices that are available to you. Throughout life, you'll spend more time with that person than any other. It's the biggest decision you'll ever make, and it deserves your best effort.

● It is a mistake to marry a project – someone who has serious problems – hoping to fix him or her. Also, marrying someone out of pity, as an act of charity, or just because you are proposed to, is not a good idea.

● Marrying someone is not like buying something from a department store with a money-back guarantee. Marriage is for keeps, and that's the way you want to approach it. If you make a wise choice, and work at it, it has the potential of getting better and better with each passing day. You wouldn't want to give it up and start all over again, for anything.

Having succeeded in the difficult task of finding that special someone to be your spouse, you now start on your equally challenging journey through life together as a married couple. The following chapters aim to give you the insights, tools and techniques to help you make your marriage the very best and most rewarding aspect of your life.

PART three

NURTURING MARRIAGE

Marriage is not the end of love, as cynics say – it is only the beginning of love. There is no need to let something beautiful – something that starts with great energy and hope – just wither and die. The pair can not only keep it alive, they can make it thrive by following some simple practices. It is vital to know how to communicate, know what problems to avoid, and keep up healthy communication. Understanding what love is and doing things to nurture it keeps the bond strong and the relationship exciting. Realizing that each has certain legitimate needs that the other should help to meet is the foundation for a lasting relationship. These requirements for a successful marriage are not difficult to meet. On the contrary, working for your marriage can be a most enjoyable part of your life.

▶ 9 ◀

CHAPTER

COMMUNICATION IN MARRIAGE

'Communication' sounds like a fashionable buzzword, but good communication is at the core of a good marriage. It is the way people transmit information, ideas, attitudes, and emotions to one another. Contrary to common belief, verbal communication through language is not the most important.[29] Non-verbal clues – tone of voice, gestures, facial expressions, bodily postures – are highly revealing.[30] Freud went so far as to say "He that has eyes to see and ears to hear may convince himself that no mortal can keep a secret. If his lips are silent, he chatters with his fingertips; betrayal oozes out of him at every pore."[31]

UNDERSTANDING COMMUNICATION

Communication is an exchange of messages. It may be in the form of saying something, such as "I love you," or expressing the same feeling through a smile, a squeeze of the hand, or a flower. Every second that you are with someone, even when you are silent and doing nothing, some sort of communication is going on.

Communication can take place at different levels and in several forms simultaneously. For example, you may say to him

"I love you" while smiling tenderly and hugging him at the same time. This is sending the same message by several methods for maximum effect – affirmation of love in three ways. People also say things that they don't really mean, or mean something and pretend that they don't. They may also send a mixed signal, for instance by saying "no, I am not mad at all" while having a sulky look and clenched fists.

Many times couples intentionally fail to communicate their true concerns because they have learned that they should exercise strict control over their thoughts, feelings, and actions. They keep a tight lid on what is going on in their inner world. Fear of expressing true feelings that are held to be taboo, or fear of being punished or rejected, often compels people to disguise things.

In marriage, after a while, even some disguised messages can be deciphered by the spouse. But it is not a good idea to bank too much on the partner's decoding talents, because this type of communication leaves much room for misinterpretation and distortion. It also reveals the absence of full trust between the couple.

FIVE OBSTACLES TO COMMUNICATION

Here are five barriers to good communication.

- *Honest misunderstanding.* What we intend to get across to others may be taken as something very different. The problem is with the human mind and the way it works, for each of us interprets what we hear and see in the privacy of our own minds, sometimes under fuzzy conditions. Also, words mean different things to different people and not everyone is equally competent in choosing the right words to express themselves perfectly. The combination can create confusion and misunderstanding.
- *Disguising the message.* We contribute to the difficulty by intentionally disguising our message – saying something while meaning something else. For instance, we may pretend that loud television noise is not bothersome, hoping that the other person will see through our disguised message.

• *Misinterpreting the message.* This happens when the other person reads something that is not there and omits to take what is there at its face value. For instance, you may say to yourself, "She is just saying that. She actually means to tell me . . ."

• *Poor self-expression.* There are times that we don't express ourselves clearly, either through laziness or a desire to be vague – as seen in statements such as, "You know what I mean," or "I'll let you figure that out." There are instances where we use a phrase as a short cut. Equally often, it is used because we just expect the listener to read our minds better than we can express our own thoughts.

• *Being confused.* Sometimes, we ourselves don't even know what we want. So we broadcast mixed signals, perhaps in an effort to clear the fog in our own minds, perhaps hoping that the other sees through the fog better than we can. In the meantime, we create confusion. "Suit the action to the word, the word to the action" is good advice from Shakespeare. Be consistent and clear. There are times when we think out loud – processing our thoughts and feelings in the presence of someone else. They may take this as trying to tell them something and a great deal of confusion is often the result.

GOOD COMMUNICATION

The effectiveness of communication between a couple is an excellent gauge of their marriage. And communication is much more than just talking. A lot of talking sometimes communicates very little. In other instances, a word or two will convey everything. Couples, after a while, develop their own 'couplese' – a set of private words, codes, and symbols.

Through verbal, gestural, and behavioral communication, much more than just the exchange of information takes place; ties of affection can also be either strengthened or weakened. Understanding not only what is being said, but the feelings behind it makes real communication possible. Here are some tips for good communication.

• *Give the other person the benefit of the doubt.* Always, even when you are certain about what they 'meant,' give them the benefit of the doubt. By so doing, you guard against misinterpreting, you create an opportunity for them to correct or reverse themselves without loss of face, and you prevent the incident from escalating into a nasty situation.

● *Keep the information flowing in both directions.* A one-way flow is limited and can be misunderstood in the absence of feedback. It is not appropriate for relationships between equals. Good communication in marriage never involves giving a lecture, issuing orders, and proclaiming non-negotiable demands. A good marriage thrives on feedback, consultation, and on mutual exchange. This mutual exchange is possible where the parties genuinely respect each other, value each other's feelings and views, and care about the quality of their thriving relationship. It is the communication of equals, of those who share their feelings.

● *Tact and kindness.* Always try to get your message across with tact and kindness. Even when you have to be critical – temper it. For instance, when someone is annoying you, you can react in several ways. You can say, "please don't do that," with a smile. Or, a sharp "don't," or even use harsh words to express your disapproval. It is always best to choose the kindest and most tactful way. Usually it works well and doesn't damage the relationship.

● *Good timing.* We often neglect timing. When we have something on our minds, we tend to unload at the earliest opportunity. But the earliest opportunity may be the wrong time to do it. It is a bad idea to want to talk with your spouse about something troublesome when she or he is in a stressed condition. To do so is not only inconsiderate, it is unwise.

It is said that the reward for patience is infinite. Why? Because it is so hard to be patient. In marriage, being patient pays handsome dividends. Wait, if you can – bear the burden a little longer. The right time is just around the corner. An added benefit of not being impulsive is that while you wait the situation may resolve itself and obviate the need for discussion.

● *Good news.* Life is not always fun and full of great news. People like to share news, and it is easy to get into the habit of blurting bad news at anyone who will listen. We do this partly because it is the bad news that usually has news value and partly because there is so much of it around.

Unless it is necessary, don't become the bearer of bad news. Because, particularly if you overdo it, soon you yourself become bad news to your spouse. He or she, consciously or unconsciously, may come to dread it every time you open your mouth. So, do the reverse. Work hard at being the bearer of good news – things that cheer your partner. Then, you'll look forward to each other's news, interactions, and communication.

● *Complaining*. Some marriages become a mutual complaining chorus. Somehow, the couple gets into the habit of complaining about everything. To some people it sounds so sophisticated, so chic, so superior – just to knock down everything and everyone. There is a lot of bitterness, criticism, and plain suffering in what they say and what they seem to feel. To these people, this is a way of life – pitching one's tent in the dump of life, by choice! Continually complaining – either about each other or the world – is a terrible practice that replaces the joy of life with bitterness and transforms communication into a harangue of negative commentary.

● *Keeping the lines open*. Just about everything can wait, when one of you needs to talk. Be always willing, even glad to listen. These occasions are like little bumps in the road that need immediate patching for the marriage to move along. If these little potholes of the mind are not attended to right away, soon the road becomes impassable and the chasm between the two of you is unbridgeable.

It is absolutely essential that husband and wife take the risk of bringing their feelings out into the open if they are to find successful ways to deal with the inevitable differences in even the best of marriages. Never assume that your partner knows what you are feeling. Even people who have lived together for years can be amazingly unaware of things that are bothering their mates or of changes in values and needs with the passing years. Keep the lines of communication open to allow closeness to continue to grow.

For every privilege there is a price tag. For the open and unrestricted access to the ear, mind and heart of your spouse, the price tag is consideration and care. Make sure that you do not abuse the privilege. Just because your partner is willing to listen, don't overdo it. Know when you are dumping and stop, long before the other is being stressed.

● *Being a confidant.* You can't communicate your innermost private feelings and thoughts to someone you can't trust. In marriage, all information is privileged communication. No spouse should ever use the information against the other, no matter how tempting it may be. Or share it with others without the partner's consent.

The life of wife and husband is a journey of togetherness, of growth, of common sharing, tears, and joys. The trust must never be violated, no matter how serious the case may be. Of course there are instances when corrective actions have to be taken. Even in these instances the pair should be able to count on their partnership – in good times and in bad times.

● *Unblocking communication.* There are times when tempers flare, emotions are high, much is said, but amazingly little is communicated. In these instances, usually one of the partners is upset about something and may unleash a confused barrage. A natural tendency for the other is to jump in with both feet and make the situation truly explosive. We suggest that you keep the word SPAR in mind particularly for these episodes.

- S = Stop for a moment
- P = Perceive what is wrong with the communication
- A = Adjust accordingly
- R = Resume communication

● *Be a spouse, not a boss.* Avoid the bossiness trap. It can so easily establish itself and poison the relationship. You are not your spouse's boss, not his or her parent, mentor, superior, or any such thing. So fight the tendency to tell each other what to do and giving orders at every turn.

Many women consider the internal matters of the home to be their turf – this is 'micropower'. Men, meanwhile, view matters of the larger world as their male arena – 'macropower'.

Based on this flawed and out-dated assumption, they defend their territories as soon as either one of them intrudes or infringes on the other's area of expertise.

The wife should assume that her husband is every bit as capable as she is in doing domestic chores, and the husband should believe that she is equally good at traditionally male-only activities. Operating from these ground rules eliminates the deadly old practice of arbitrary assumptions, role assignment based on gender, and jockeying for dominance.

THE SEVEN DO'S OF GOOD LISTENING

As well as having so much on our minds that we like to unload, humans are notorious talkers. People love the echo of their own voices – but not echoes vibrating in solitude. There has to be a listener, an audience. In marriage, neither spouse should become exclusively a talker or a listener. Both of you should be each other's caring listener on a fair and equal basis. Take turns. Be each other's resident therapist – letting out the worries and concerns of your beloved and making room for the unavoidable ones lurking around the next bend. So learn to become a good listener by adopting the practices listed below.

- *Listen caringly*. Everyone has so much on their minds. The burden seems heavy and must be unloaded regularly. But there are few people who are willing to be loving listeners. Make sure that you are the best and the most willing uncritical listener that your spouse could possibly find. Don't let the bartender do it, don't leave it to strangers. Not even friends should take your place.
- *Listen with your body*. Turn fully toward the person who is doing the talking and get rid of all distractions. Assume a welcoming posture and concentrate on the speaker.
- *Listen with your eyes*. Establish eye-to-eye contact. Trustingly and caringly invite him or her to feel free to take the necessary time to share feelings and thoughts. Look for non-verbal cues in facial expressions, gestures, and posture. As Mark Twain said, "Man is the only animal that blushes. Or needs to." There is a lot of information in the face and the eyes.

● *Listen with your ears.* Hear what the speaker is really saying. Be alert to the meanings as well as the intensity and tone of the words.

● *Listen with your heart.* Feel the emotions of the speaker. Is he or she angry, pleased, disappointed, fearful, frustrated? As observant as the eyes and the ears are, we should also remember the Chinese proverb, "Two-thirds of what we see is behind our eyes."

● *Listen with your mouth closed.* Allow his or her cup to empty. This is the wrong time for impatience, interruption, or instant solutions. When people talk, frequently all they want is an empathetic and understanding listener.

● *Validate and confirm the message.* Make the 'airing-out' an even greater success. When the speaker is through, you may want to confirm your perception of the situation to be certain it is correct by saying, "You seem so happy about your plan," or "I can see that this is making you frustrated and angry," or "Am I right in thinking that you really don't want to go?" This will help you and the speaker to have a meeting of the minds on the issue and forms the basis for your joint understanding or decision.

THE SEVEN DON'TS OF GOOD LISTENING

'Don'ts' are just as important as 'do's.' To be a good listener, you must avoid at least the seven temptations listed below.

● *Don't interrupt.* Let the speaker complete the thought and fully express himself or herself.

● *Don't contradict.* Allow others to have their own opinions; everyone is entitled to their views and feelings. You don't have to agree with what is said, but there is no need to do all you can to prove someone foolish for thinking and feeling the way they do. A relationship is a two-way street. You want to be listened to, tolerated, and even loved? Then be prepared to offer the same to others.

● *Don't criticize or lecture about past behavior.* If a mistake was made, allow others to see it for themselves during the conversation. This will enable them to learn their own lessons from the experience with much less embarrassment. Try to keep their self-esteem intact as much as possible. Marriage should never become a place where a thick dossier is kept – a dossier on your partner to pull out on every occasion and show him or her the evidence of past follies.

● *Don't nod your head constantly*. Nodding in approval once in a while is encouraging, but doing it too frequently can be annoying and disruptive. It can also imply boredom, or "Yeah, yeah, I know – I heard it all before . . . don't waste my time . . . get to the end of it."

● *Don't assume what is said is the total content of the message*. Watch carefully for clues in tone and body language for what might be really bothering someone. With a few carefully worded comments or a gentle question, the whole story may come tumbling out, to their own surprise.

● *Don't interrogate or patronize*. When your partner is in a bad mood, you need to be particularly careful not to interrogate – that is, ask probing questions that aim to prove him or her wrong. These are times for just being there, understanding and empathizing. Avoid questioning as much as possible. Particularly resist asking questions such as, "But did you try to see why your boss got mad at you? – what do you think you did that made her mad?" or, "It can't be the way you say it. It just doesn't make sense. Now, tell me, did you have your facts straight?" Don't ever say things such as, "Now, if I were you, I would have handled it differently," or "You ought to be more circumspect next time."

● *Don't use the occasion for self-aggrandizement*. This is no time to show how great you are by such things as trying to top the story or anecdote with a better one from your own past. Don't try to improve on someone's jokes – just enjoy being his or her audience.

GENDER AND COMMUNICATION

There are differences in the communication patterns of women and men.[32] For example, folklore says that women are more adept than men in interpreting non-verbal communication – they are better judges of voice tones, facial expressions, body language – things that cannot be put into words. Research shows that this belief is correct.[33] So if your husband is not as intuitive as you are, he may simply be a victim of his gender rather than being insensitive.

Finally, a good closing note is the saying of Zeno of Citium, "The reason we have two ears and only one mouth is that we may listen the more and talk the less."

▶10◀

CHAPTER

LOVE IN MARRIAGE

We all talk about love and think we know what we mean by it. But few of us have exactly the same notion about love. Why? Because love is an emotion – a feeling. And like all feelings, love is hard to describe and has a large element that is unique to the person who feels it. Love is a mixture of attraction, admiration, and respect. It is valuing someone or something. It can take different forms. It can be limited or broad, primitive or mature. In certain cases love is so powerful and total that it is called *adoration* – particularly when there is an element of worship, and perhaps a touch of irrationality. At other times it is a fantasy feeling called *infatuation*. Whatever love is, it truly makes the world go around.

IS LOVE ESSENTIAL FOR MARRIAGE?

Love is not essential for marriage. There are other reasons for marriage – such as financial considerations, the desire to have children, the need for companionship, and social pressures. Also, there are many marriages that later become loveless.

Staying married – just like getting married – can be motivated by a variety of considerations, other than being in love – not having a viable alternative, concern for the children, the social stigma of divorce, financial risks, lack of courage to venture into a new relationship, honoring the pledge, "Till death us do part," and so forth.

But staying married under these circumstances is hardly having a successful marriage! There is no need at all for any marriage to end up in this sorry state. If there was enough love to get you married in the first place, then there is no reason why that love should die. Some feel that marriage is the death of love, but these are people who don't know how to nurture love, or don't want to keep on earning it. To our mind, love in marriage is priceless. It is worth the effort that it takes to keep the fire of love very much aflame.

LOVE OF PEOPLE FOR PEOPLE

The American psychiatrist Harry Stack Sullivan writes, "When the satisfaction or the security of another person becomes as significant to one as is one's own satisfaction or security, then the state of love exists."[34] We like this definition with a slight modification – when the satisfaction of another becomes as significant or more significant to one than one's own satisfaction, then love exists. We prefer this definition because satisfaction also includes security. More importantly, it accounts for acts of love that sacrifice one's own security and satisfaction for another. For example, when parents forgo their own satisfaction for a child's.

Psychologist Robert J. Sternberg has studied love and concludes that "Love may feel, subjectively, like a single emotion, but it is in fact composed of a number of different components."[35] He lists these components as:

1. Promoting the welfare of the loved one.
2. Experiencing happiness with the loved one.
3. High regard for the loved one.
4. Being able to count on the loved one in times of need.
5. Mutual understanding of the loved one.
6. Sharing oneself and one's things with the loved one.
7. Receiving emotional support from the loved one.
8. Giving emotional support to the loved one.
9. Intimate communication with the loved one.
10. Valuing the loved one in one's own life.

Sternberg dissects love into ten ingredients of feelings, thoughts, and dispositions. Regardless of its bits and pieces, love is both the magnet that attracts the pair and the force that holds them together. For a successful marriage, it is not enough to fall in love and get married. It is a good start, but what is needed is for this love to become stronger with time. This won't happen automatically. In fact, neglect and taking each other for granted can be deadly to love – leaving behind only a pile of ashes. Also, as Shakespeare reminds us, "The course of true love never did run smooth." It takes constant care and work to keep the fire well stocked.

CAPACITY FOR LOVE

Love is the engine of a good marriage. The capacity to love has its germ within everyone. In the very young, love is basically limited to the self. One has to learn to love others.

People have different capacities for love as well as different things that they love. In spite of these differences there are many similarities. For instance, it is easy to love someone who is very agreeable, those who make us feel good, or anyone who does things for us. This is self-limited or self-confined love. Narcissus reportedly looked in the mirror at his hunched back and proclaimed admiringly, "It looks good. After all, it is on me." But the capacity to love must go beyond self-limited love. In a successful marriage, both self-affirming love and the love for the spouse combine into a shared love – the intertwining of the two into one inseparable loving whole.

TYPES OF LOVE

Five types of love are discussed below.

- *Basic love.* This is the undeveloped raw material that we start with in life. It is exclusive to oneself. In this form of love – typical of early childhood – even your affection for the most beloved person in your life, your parent, is motivated by what she or he does for you. She feeds you, cleans you, and makes you feel good. You love her because she is a powerful extension of yourself, and ministers to all your needs. An invisible cord still ties you to her.

A variety of basic love is seen in animals, particularly between infants and mothers. For instance, an elephant calf follows its mother incessantly; a baby chimp clings to her mother for dear life. The bond is strong between such pairs. Even when the mother elephant is dying of thirst – spread on the dry soil – she allows the calf to continue sucking at her udder for the last drops of milk. This is the order of nature. The mother gives of herself to the last drop and the calf eagerly takes it – reflecting the fundamental nature of self-love, which finds expression most clearly in animals and young children. It is nature's way of enhancing the survival chances of the young.

● *Kinship love*. This is the next higher level of love – extending positive feelings to those who meet your needs, support you, feel like you do, look like you, are related to you, share the same set of values, or have other things in common with you. You are still the pivot around which these people or things revolve. Many people's capacity to love extends only this far.

● *Altruistic love*. The next level involves the capacity for loving without much regard to any obvious self-centered considerations – loving people or things for what they are. Love of ideas and principles, love of nature and animals, or love of children in general are some examples.

● *Emotional love*. A form of love dominated by emotion involves projecting one's hopes and dreams on what seems to be a perfect person. When this emotional infatuation leads to marriage, after a time the day-to-day difficulties of life will inevitably burst the bubble. Something more substantial must then replace the dream-like quality of emotional love if the relationship is to thrive.

The couple must then draw on other emotional, intellectual, spiritual and physical resources to remain attached. When they do, they can actually fall even deeper in love as they make the necessary efforts to change from being in love with an ideal to loving a real human being – complete with faults and limitations.

Both puppy love and mature love may go through the emotional phase and it may be hard to distinguish between a relationship that will endure a lifetime and one that is as temporary as a spring flower. This is where caution comes in; unless other attractions are also present, a decision to marry based solely on one's emotions is not wise. Only a relationship built on a solid basis of genuine compatibility and respect will last when the starry-eyed phase passes.

● *Marriage love*. Healthy marriage includes all of the above loves – you marry someone because you expect good things; you also love your spouse, because of kinship; you love your partner just for what he or she is, and you love her or him for crazy reasons.

A solid marriage has a particularly large measure of altruistic love – the stand-alone love that involves loving people for what they are and not only for what they do for you. It is said that, "Love is blind; friendship closes its eyes." That's the kind of affectional bond that loving couples have – they are lovers and they are friends too. And, as Woodrow Wilson has said, "You cannot be friends upon any other terms than upon the terms of equality."

Marriage love is also a pragmatic love when the couple trust and love each other because of what they do for one another and in spite of the peculiarities and quirks that each may have. Research shows that we tend to like those who are similar to us.[36] This attraction is called *homogamy* and its impact is seen in the practice of like marrying like. Attraction to people who are like us is not limited to physical similarity. Intellectual compatibility, similar religious and cultural beliefs, and a shared sense of humor are also important.

UNCONDITIONAL LOVE

Is there such a thing as unconditional love – the kind of love that has no conditions attached to it? If it does exist, it is rare indeed, particularly in adult relationships. Parents and children sometimes seem to show this type of unconditional love towards each other – for instance, when parents endure extraordinary hardships and suffering to care for their mentally or physically handicapped children; or when a child spends most of his or her life diligently caring for an invalid parent. But it is impossible to prove that these instances represent unconditional love. The sense of duty, deriving satisfaction from caring, and other factors may be operating in these situations. In our view, love is at its best when it's based on free choice, when it's an earned, reciprocal love.

We first experience love in our parents' home. The genetic link between parents and children is a basis for forming a strong bond. This bond is strengthened by a variety of factors, such as the father seeing his own gifts reflected in his son, or the mother seeing her little girl as an opportunity to work for and give all those things that she herself wanted and never achieved.

Also, it is easier for your parents and siblings to accept and love you as you are because you are much more like them in your temperament, actions, and values. Recent studies show that our genes have a major influence in determining temperaments – qualities that were previously thought to be largely dependent on the environment.[37]

Your spouse is not only the product of different genetic material, but has also been raised, educated, and trained by different parents, and may have different expectations and standards from yours. In marriage, each spouse must continually earn the love and acceptance of the other. It is not the same automatic love and acceptance that you might have enjoyed in the parental home. Unconditional love, if it ever exists, does not come with the marriage license – the common vow, "To love and to cherish," notwithstanding.

Once you regularly earn your love, then some of it can be saved and drawn upon at times of need. When we are growing up, we may receive unconditional love from our parents, grandparents, and even siblings. When we get married, we expect unconditional love. Our attitude is "Love me no matter what I do or say – love me just the way I am". But expecting unearned love in an adult situation is foolish. It won't be forthcoming – we have to earn it. We are now adults and others have a right to expect adult behavior from us; we must shape up and grow up and not expect others to love us automatically.

One of the difficult adjustments of going from one's childhood home to one's marital home is this transition from automatic to earned respect and love. After many years of earning love and respect – years of unselfishly being there for each other through all kinds of hardships – the couple has paid its dues and can eventually grow into a solid, firmly anchored, consistent love. Even then their love should not be taken for granted. Yet unconditional love – love that must be given no matter how the spouse behaves – has its place. When the beloved develops physical or mental incapacities that limit his or her capacity to reciprocate, the healthy spouse will shoulder the load with the full realization that he or she would have received the same faithful love in a similar situation.

▸ 11 ◂

CHAPTER

THE PSYCHOLOGY OF ATTRACTION

No human being is perfect. Every one of us is a combination of pluses and minuses. We may find ourselves attracted to someone because that person's net score in our estimation is a big plus. We are repelled by another, because his net score seems to us very negative. We are attracted to people, things, and events that make us feel good – and repelled by those that threaten us physically, or offend us psychologically. The degree of attraction or repulsion changes over time, because we ourselves are constantly changing – and our likes and dislikes are part of this ever-changing process. Also, our circumstances are always changing – sometimes dramatically, sometimes subtly, but always changing nonetheless. These changes, from within and without, clearly impact on what we are, how we feel, and the value we place on people and things.

The attraction of one human being to another depends on the perceiver's own condition and the setting against which the other person is evaluated. For instance, after an exceptionally harrowing day even the beautiful song of a cardinal may be annoying. When we are in a great mood, by contrast, even an insult is taken good-humoredly.

Barring the extremes of mood and in the course of normal

daily fluctuations, the relationship between two people evolves gradually – for the better or for the worse. This is particularly the case with husbands and wives. They spend so much time with each other, and their lives are so intimately intertwined. Within this relationship the degree of attraction between the two of them is the best measure of the marriage's success.

THE PHYSICAL EXPRESSION OF LOVE

There is an endless obsession with sex today. The search for 'perfect sex' is all-consuming to many people. There is a feeling among some that their sex lives are not satisfactory, or at least not as good as other people's. These dissatisfactions are largely due to exaggerated expectations, immature fantasies, and the failure to follow simple wholesome practices. Making love, when stripped of all its psychological baggage, is as natural as breathing – just as vital and just as problem-free.

The secret of having satisfactory sex is in toning down expectations, and maintaining a loving relationship. Couples seeking sex therapy often have difficulties in resolving conflict and in expressing physical and emotional intimacy.[38] The following factors influence erotic love in marriage.

- *Old paradigm mentality*. Under the old paradigm women were expected to be submissive sexually. Women were viewed and treated as objects – givers of pleasure, not receivers of it. Men took pleasure without thinking of women's feelings.
- *New paradigm outlook*. Women are equally entitled to full enjoyment in love-making. Men should take pride in being a source of pleasure to their partners. Mutual enjoyment is much superior to a one-person party.
- *Psychological hocus pocus*. Freudian-type speculations are often mistaken as facts, and fancy-sounding, yet baseless, psychologizing is a popular sport. Failure to recognize the beauty and legitimacy of the sex impulse in marriage can be a major problem. Seeing erotic love as an overt expression of supposed hidden neurotic tendencies – such as wanting to inflict pain or vanquish someone – is little more than the figment of a sick imagination.

● *Sex as power play*. Women, traditionally powerless, tended to use denial of sex as a way of exercising power. The historical episode in Athens when women denied sex to their husbands unless they ended the war is an example.

● *Sex and male chauvinism*. Men also use sex to demonstrate their virility, manhood, and dominance – a vestige of bygone times when primitive men were more like beasts than humans.

● *Rigidity and lack of spontaneity*. Assuming certain standards for sex and being unimaginative in the act itself – such as making love only in a certain way or in a specific place – reflect lack of spontaneity. Every couple is a small kingdom unto itself and the pair are the rulers and rule-makers of their kingdom.

When making love, the pair should put all their inhibitions and preconceptions aside and become fully responsive to each other's mood and desire. There is only one rule that the couple must follow – a complete sharing of their gifts for the fullest satisfaction of both.

● *Complacency and carelessness*. Taking each other for granted and not caring about maintaining attractiveness can be deadly to making love. Lack of personal hygiene and a mechanical attitude of going through the motions diminishes pleasure. So put a little effort, a bit of care, and a large touch of tenderness into it and the experience will remain as rewarding as ever.

● *Taboos and embarrassment*. For whatever reason, many taboos are associated with erotic love – even in marriage. People are embarrassed to talk about, much less tell each other their intimate feelings and preferences. So a wife may go through years of marriage sexually frustrated, simply because she could not bring herself to tell her husband how she wanted to be treated during love-making. The husband may develop impotency because he is embarrassed to suggest a more stimulating approach.

● *Fearing failure*. Both husband and wife may have their own fears regarding failure to satisfy either each other or themselves. These fears, in themselves, can become self-fulfilling prophecies. Human sexuality, although biologically provided for, is very susceptible to psychological influences. Fears of failure may precipitate frigidity and impotency.

● *Anxiety and worries*. Taking the worries and concerns of daily life into love-making is like dragging a dead cat to a banquet. Learn to set aside the cares of the day and give yourself fully to the pleasures of sex. Put everything else on hold and attend to the pleasure of shared love. There are times when long-standing stress is involved; stress and making love seldom go hand in hand. And men and women often require different methods of dealing with stress.[39]

● *Foreplay, shared play, and postplay*. When it comes to making love, men and women have different needs and preferences. Men generally prefer to get to it, be done, and roll over and sleep. Women generally prefer a period of foreplay marked by loving words, hugs, and touching. It takes a while for them to get into the mood for the main course. Then, afterward, they like dessert – a period of affectional exchanges and kissing, before rolling over and going to sleep. There are always exceptions to these general rules – and all of them are legitimate. Remember that love-making is the shared play of two equal partners. The husband and the wife should strike their own preferred compromise that allows both to have a most rewarding experience.

● *Sex-limited affection*. Some couples are only affectionate during sex and seldom bother to hold hands, kiss, or hug at other times. Men are more prone to this type of compartmentalized affection than women. Some men may feel or act affectionately only when they want sex. Having their desire satisfied, they revert to their usual aloofness till the next time. This is hardly the all-encompassing love relationship of two mutually devoted individuals. It is more like a con game.

● *Health, nutrition, and rest*. Good health and nutritious diet are important to satisfactory sex. So is being physically rested. Making love in the late evening, for instance, is not smart for a couple exhausted from a long day of work and chores.

● *Habituation and monotony*. This is the biggest troublemaker. In many instances the original fire of desire gives way to boredom, monotony, and lack of interest. It is at this point that others begin to look more inviting than one's spouse – the grass seems greener on the other side of the fence, so to speak. Men are especially prone to this trap, which can cause much heartache, infidelity, and divorce. One way to guard against this potential marriage-buster is to keep your sexual sharing as exciting and rewarding as realistically possible.

● *Love and life*. The relationship of a couple is an entity in its own right. Everything that happens to them and between them has an impact on it. A constant adding and subtracting goes on both consciously and unconsciously. Any good thing that you do adds to the strength of the relationship and will spill over into other facets of your life together. A kindly remark at breakfast may in fact be the continuation of deeply satisfying sex of the night before, which in turn will lead to other affectionate exchanges and more satisfying sex. This is a sort of self-propagating loop – a good relationship goes a long way toward insuring satisfying sex. And satisfying sex contributes significantly to the quality of the relationship.

● *Dating after marriage*. Should one stop dating after marriage? We strongly recommend that you keep on dating. With one condition: now, you date only your spouse. Why should dating stop with marriage? Remember the delicious times that you had during your courtship? When you used to put your fine clothes on, go to nice places to eat and dance? Well, keep on doing it. Make sure that you find time to do it. If you could find time during your courtship, you can find time in marriage. All your obligations must give a little so that the two of you can carry on a lifetime of courtship.

● *Accommodating children*. The arrival of children should not signal the end of the honeymoon for the couple. Be smart. With a little ingenuity, you can enjoy the gift of your children without giving up your romance. The love of children is no substitute for the love between the two of you – and they are not incompatible.

● *Avoiding ruts*. Habits and routines are economical ways of doing things that come up time and again. That's the way the human mind handles routines efficiently. But ruts and routines when applied to your love life lead to boredom and dissatisfaction. So avoid getting into a rut. Surprise each other, from time to time, with a new idea. Novelty brings excitement and freshness to the relationship. Be creative and allow yourselves the freedom of exploring each other's gifts. Take our word for it, there is absolutely nothing wrong with enjoying your gifts to the maximum. That's what a successful marriage is all about.

● *Establishing a routine*. As undesirable as lack of spontaneity is in making love, establishing certain positive routine cues may be helpful. They become associated with pleasurable memories and enhance the enjoyment of love-making.

HOW TO KEEP AND ENHANCE YOUR LOVE

When you fall in love, there are always reasons for it. Maybe the looks, the sharp mind or the sense of humor sparked the feeling. Possibly money, the feeling of security or the attention you received – or any combination of the above and other factors – played some role. The important thing is that you are in love, you are married, and you want to prove to the cynical that marriage is not the death of love. Here are some do's and don'ts to keep in mind.

● *Working*. Don't take your love for granted. Always work for it. If you do, it keeps on getting better and better; it is worth the effort. Celebrate your togetherness by doing things that endear you to each other.

● *Capitalizing*. What were the things that he or she found appealing about you? "My looks – and how can you keep the same looks when ageing is unavoidable?" you say. Well, getting old and getting unattractive are two different things. There is no reason to get careless. Right diet, exercise, some attention to personal appearance, and a positive mental attitude go a long way in keeping you attractive.

Also, the best-kept secret of marriage is that both of you age together and neither of you really notices the gradual changes in physical appearance. You could look as appealing to each other as you did on day one!

● *Sharing*. Make sure that you are an equal partner – not only when it comes to privileges, but also in contributions. What are you bringing to the partnership? Anything at all? Do you generate income? Is that all you do, leaving the rest of the chores as your spouse's duties?

Make a list of your contributions to make sure that you are contributing your fair share to the joint venture. Don't use it as a bargaining tool or to show off. The two of you can consult on how each of you can contribute even more meaningfully to your relationship.

● *Delivering*. Love is a positive feeling based on real and imaginary things that we put together in our head. Marriage is one big testing ground of mental notions. So, in the proving ground of marriage, you need to make adjustments – junking unrealistic expectations as well as meeting the realistic ones. You can make your marriage a true love-nest by doing things for each other – delivering what is cherished, expected, and reasonable. A partner who is a loafer, who is there for the ride, will soon end up loveless and even abandoned.

● *Admiring*. Be the number-one fan and supporter of your spouse – it makes her or him feel good and helps in developing and strengthening good qualities. Remember Shakespeare's advice, "Love's best habit is a soothing tongue."

● *Criticizing*. So far as possible, don't criticize. Even when it is absolutely necessary, take your time and do it with the greatest tact. This doesn't mean that you are not being candid and honest. You are being considerate. People mistake rudeness, insensitivity, and abusiveness for candor. Don't be rash. You can always be as rude as you want, later.

● *Giving*. Learn the joy of giving. It works wonders:

> Giving returns to the giver;
> Blessings come back to the one who blesses;
> And love sent out circles back in some way to its source.[40]

● *Receiving*. Marriage is a true give and take. Graciously accepting kindness and favors is just as important as generously giving. There is great satisfaction in having one's offer of love, gifts and kindness accepted with appreciation. So, let him do the little and big things for you and, in turn, you do the same for him.

● *Bonding*. Find common ground and mutual interests. Don't jump to conclusions that you don't like this or that which he or she likes. You paint yourself into a corner, if you do – and you'll have to live up to your assertions to save face, if for no other reason. Besides, marriage is about building greater and greater common links; it is not only a parallel existence of convenience. If you genuinely try, you are bound to find many things that you both like to do together. There is a spill-over effect – the more things you love in common, the stronger your love for each other.

● *Communicating*. Keep the communication lines open. Make sure that you share with each other your concerns, worries, hopes, goals, dreams, and all those things that please or irritate you. Yet, do this with loving care. Don't abuse this privilege. You certainly want to talk about everything freely with the number-one person in your life, but you don't want to unload everything on him or her. If you are inconsiderate, soon all the bad things that you unload will do two things – your spouse becomes burdened and you become the bearer of bad vibes. The result is weakening or even loss of love. Also heed Shakespeare's advice, "They do not love that do not show their love."

● *Surprising*. Pleasant surprises are like an oxygen-bearing breeze to the fire of love. Take him out to his favorite restaurant when he is least expecting it. Bring her a bouquet of flowers not because it is her birthday or anniversary – simply because it is a special day just to be married to her.

● *Respecting*. It is hard to imagine any two people being more intimate than a husband and wife. Yet this intimacy should not be taken as a license for loss of respect. Being respected is being valued for what one is. It is as important as being loved.

● *Making-up*. Don't let grievances pile up. When there is a disagreement or hurt feeling, resolve it lovingly right away. Don't ever pick up your pillow and spend the night on the couch. It is the most human – yet the most stupid – thing to do. You'll have a miserable night on the couch being both mad and uncomfortable. Besides, even the little hurts, when not gotten rid of, multiply inside you like germs. They will surely poison you, the one you love and the relationship.

On any given occasion, someone must take the initiative and make the first move toward reconciliation. And this is the hardest and most dangerous part. It is hard because of pride, ego, and the feeling that it was all his or her fault. To get over this block, you can tell your spouse something to the effect that, "I don't want us to stay angry about this because we must not allow anything – even temporarily – to get between us. I value our love and if it takes a little swallowing of my pride to protect it – well, I'll do it. It really doesn't matter whose fault it is. The important thing is not to let it get between us." You can always say and mean it sincerely, "I am sorry I made you angry."

The quick apology is a wonderful thing that both of you must initiate. Neither of you should be the one always to apologize first, because it can set a bad pattern – one partner making all first moves towards reconciliation while the other holds out. You have to be careful. Always make up quickly and make sure that neither side comes out injured or defeated from the scrimmage.

MARRIAGE LOVE QUOTIENT TEST

Here is a simple test for the condition of your marriage love. Give yourself a score for each question:

0 = Never
1 = Once in a while
3 = Often
5 = Always

	SCORE
1. My spouse is affectionate toward me.	___
2. My heart misses a beat when I look at him/her.	___
3. I would rather spend time with him/her than be with others.	___
4. After love-making, I feel satisfaction and content ment.	___
5. I consider my spouse as my best friend.	___
6. I can talk to my spouse openly.	___
7. I think that marrying him/her was a great decision.	___
8. My spouse understands me.	___
9. My spouse still does all kinds of things to please me.	___
10. I have pleasant thoughts about my spouse.	___
TOTAL SCORE	___

If your total score is:

0–8 = There is very little spark in your marriage.
9–18 = There is enough love to build on.
19–40 = There is a lot of love in your marriage.
41–50 = Congratulations! Your marriage is made in heaven.

▶ 12 ◀

CHAPTER

NEED SATISFACTION

Human beings have a limited number of needs – but numerous wants that are generated by our desires. As a rule, the greater the number of wants, the greater the unhappiness and emptiness of the person's life. We should keep wants in check. Need satisfaction is the bedrock of marriage, and it is in marriage that the couple can best satisfy many of each other's physical and psychological needs. Studies show that we find others attractive to the extent that they seem to meet our needs. There are four classes of needs – physical, emotional, psychological, and spiritual.

GENDER AND NEEDS

Biology and culture make the sexes different in their need profile. Women, for example, are reported to have a greater need for acceptance and affiliation than men.[41] This difference is neither good nor bad. It just exists. Its recognition goes a long way in avoiding problems in the relationship. Also, women usually have a greater need both to express themselves verbally and to hear their partner speak his mind. Women have always been the pivot for socializing, bonding, and educating the species. They are the main networkers. Men, on the other hand, are less verbal. Men tend to keep things inside, do less talking, have poorer speaking skills, and become impatient under verbal demand.

SELF-INTEREST

Self-interest is at the core of human motivation, and is the driving force in life. The individual is, in a real sense, the center of the universe. So it is the most natural thing for us to look after our own interests. Questions such as "What's in it for me? How does it affect me? Where do I stand in this case? How can I get more out of this?" are legitimate questions. Marriage is not exempt from these considerations. Here are two individuals – each trying to maximize their gains at a minimum cost to themselves. The challenge facing marriage is to accept this valid impulse of self-interest and strike an arrangement where both partners come out ahead in the marriage deal. Efforts should be made to meet each other's legitimate needs. It is in marriage that two individuals can have their cake and eat it too. They can successfully benefit from each other's gifts without either party being a loser.

Self-interest is a good thing, but selfishness is not. Everything that we do should be guided by enlightened self-interest. In marriage, this idea translates into something like this:

- what is good for her or him is good for the marriage; and
- what is good for the marriage is good for me.

Being generous and kind to others, being forgiving, not taking offense easily, being self-sacrificing, and so on – these are great human qualities, not easily acquired, and high ideals that few of us live up to. But at the practical level, you love her not because of her, but because of yourself. You love her because she makes you feel good, because she loves you, validates you, satisfies your needs. It is as simple as that.

Even when you forgive someone for a heinous act, you do this for a reward – within you, you feel more gratification for having forgiven than could be gained by revenge. If you want to have a great relationship with your spouse, your friend, or your boss, then do and say those things that serve their interests. What's in it for you? Friendship and reciprocity. Why do you want their friendship? Because it is in your self-interest. Simple. A wonderful thing about mature human relationships is that while we are serving someone else's interests our own self-interest is also served.

Self-interest is the maturation of selfishness. We all start out in life by being selfish. Young children have no clue about consideration for others, the sense of right and wrong, and the rule of fair play. All their actions are directed at serving the most important person in their tiny universe – themselves. This is perfectly normal at this stage of development. We hardly think of these little tots as selfish. But psychological evolution is not genetically programmed, and some people don't go much beyond childish selfishness – they age, but they don't grow. These individuals are high-risk partners, still ruled by the myopia of selfish gain.

LONG-TERM CONSIDERATIONS

As a rule, we humans are short-term investors – we prefer immediate results over those in the distant future. This short-term orientation makes sense in many instances. But marriage is for the long haul, for a long and satisfying life of togetherness. Hence, all investments in marriage should be made with an eye to years and decades ahead. Everything we do and say in marriage represents investments of various sizes and merits. So during moments of anger don't do or say things that erode your long-term investment. Even the best marriages experience instances where tempers flare. You need to cool the tempers and not use them as a fuel to burn or scorch the relationship. Each time you get angry or feel a disappointment, just look at it as a small, temporary reversal in the great fortune that you have put together – your relationship fortune. Minimize your losses by resisting the urge to attack each other. A bump in the road of your long journey of togetherness should not be allowed to become a damaging incident. Be a long-term investor.

MARRIAGE IS A WIN–WIN PROPOSITION

A good marriage is not a win or lose transaction, but a win and win relationship. To keep it that way, remember these points:

- *Your first priority is to please and satisfy your partner.* Keeping your spouse happy may sometimes require sacrificing your own wishes. But, these sacrifices are like savings – money you set aside that will pay back compound interest.
- *Reciprocation is the key.* It takes two people to make a successful marriage and reciprocity is at the heart of it. If only one of you is doing the good things, with little reciprocation from the other, resentment develops and trouble starts. So return her kindness. She will be encouraged and is much more likely to do it again.
- *Learn what you can do.* Each person has a particular set of needs. Your task is to find out how best you can meet the needs of your partner. Stay away from guesswork. Get the facts. Talk to each other and find out about the things you can do to make your special someone feel better.
- *Allow for change.* People's needs change over time. Don't keep on serving the same psychological menu. Periodically reassess what you are providing. Is it still needed? Are there some new needs? Can you help with them?
- *Men and women have different needs.* No two people's needs are exactly the same, and this is particularly true across gender differences. Women as a group may value certain things more than men do, while men may cherish other things. Always make allowances for gender preferences. They are both legitimate and important.

FINDING OUT WHAT IS REALLY IMPORTANT

"What's in it for me?" is a common question to ask – perhaps not in so many words and not even consciously. You need to make sure that you have a great deal to offer each other. Marriage is like a trading post where two people exchange goods. The greater the satisfaction of the traders, the more likely that the trade will continue. This is the basis of social exchange theory.[42]

A deadly mistake is to go by stereotypes and guesswork – reasoning that "men like such things – he is a man – therefore, he too, must like that." For instance, you might try surprising her by giving her an expensive sewing machine for her birthday or buying him a motor cycle. But she might hate sewing and he might despise riding motor cycles. Don't treat him as a generic man and don't treat her as a generic woman. Make a little effort to find out what your partner really wants. Even loving something is not necessarily wanting it; for example, a man may love chocolates but be trying hard to lose weight. His wife is not doing him a favor by buying him a box of expensive European chocolates. Instead, she could look around and see if there are low-calorie chocolates – which are still edible – that she can buy for him. This shows both love and sensitivity.

There are times when we don't reveal what we really want. We may even go through a lot of trouble and use an elaborate smoke-screen to hide what we really want. We do this particularly when what we want may verge on the taboo, reflect poorly on us, or trigger a negative reaction. We are all insecure and afraid of being discovered. Maybe she is the one who longs to own a motor cycle and do what is thought to be a man's thing. Maybe he is the one who loves sewing – something traditionally considered to be feminine. A good marriage is not chained to meaningless traditions and stereotypes. It allows itself a great deal of flexibility to meet each partner's needs. Keep in mind that you did not marry a generic type – you married a unique human being with his or her own set of needs.

● *Feelings don't have to be justified.* Personal likes and dislikes can often be respected without doing any harm to anyone. For example, if your spouse says that he hates fish, so be it. No point in trying to marshal an encyclopedia of evidence to show him why he shouldn't. Just respect it, and don't plan a dinner party featuring fish. Eat fish, if you want to, when he is out of town. When your wife says that she despises violent movies, respect that too. You don't have to remind her that it is all acting and pretending and that she should not be so uptight about something like that. She knows all those valid reasons. Just respect her opinion and don't take her to see *Rambo*.

HUMAN NEEDS

Human needs span a broad range – vital needs of safety and survival are at one end; in the middle are needs that are not so critical, yet highly necessary; and at the other end are the 'luxury' that human beings feel. The vital or basic needs are few, but life depends on meeting them: water; food; air; sex (for propagation of the species); and protection from the elements, injury, and disease. The middle range includes needs that are concerned with feelings – emotional or affectional needs: the need to love and to be loved; feeling of being accepted, valued and admired; feeling happy and contented; experiencing goodwill, kindness, and sympathy.

Then, there is a long list of psychological needs[43]: they include the need for achievement, autonomy, order, respect, affiliation, attention, understanding, relaxation, nurturance, play, creativity, acquisition, and self-actualization. Finally, there are spiritual needs: the need for transcendence – going beyond the present and the tangible; to understand and relate to a supreme being; for insight and oneness with the realm of the spirit; for prayer or meditation.

The partners in a marriage are in a position fully to satisfy some of each other's needs. A good lifelong marriage is one in which the pair strives to help each other in meeting the rest of their varied needs.

PAY ATTENTION TO YOUR SPOUSE

In the expression 'paying attention,' the operative word is 'pay,' meaning that it is going to cost you time, energy, and emotion. But you must do it all the time. The common trap of not paying needed attention to a partner is fatal to marriage. Before long, he or she becomes more like a blur in the background than the centerpiece of your life. Do all you can to avoid complacency and taking each other for granted. Make it a habit to pay attention to your spouse – to every aspect of her or him. Here is a partial list of what needs attention.

● *Eye contact*. Look in the eyes of the other person when he or she is talking to you. It gives the talker a sense of confidence, of being taken seriously, and of being worthy of your full attention. It would be even nicer not to fiddle with things, to drop whatever you are doing and sincerely focus total attention on the partner. Of course there are times when you don't and you can't do this. But make it a habit to do it whenever you can.

● *Appearance*. When she curls her hair just to look her best for you, when he shaves just to be neat on your day alone together – notice it and express your appreciation. Always be on the look-out to notice and compliment appearance. It makes her or him feel good and try to keep it up. It is a winning proposition all around.

● *Needs*. Pay attention to each other's needs. What is it that she wants and what is it that he wants? Be sensitive and pick up the cue, and help meet those needs – if you can possibly do it – even without waiting for the other to verbalize them. This kind of caring will endear you to each other and is absolutely priceless.

● *Feelings*. Pay attention to feelings. They are as important as anything. Is she hurt, in a bad mood, or sad? Is he angry, on the edge, or depressed? Also notice good moods; when she is humming to herself, when he is whistling his favorite tune. Chip in, without being disruptive, and boost the good mood. You can give the good feeling a tremendous boost, just in the same way that you can aggravate a bad mood by unwisely joining in the down-swing.

It sounds like a lot of work – having a good marriage and making it better day by day – but if you make the effort to do some of these things, you will soon do them almost automatically. Your good instincts do most of the work without too much exertion. The results are definitely worth the small amount of effort involved.

PART four

EMOTIONS & MARRIAGE

Emotions and feelings are at the heart of marriage, and marriage is a living system that can produce both good and bad feelings. It can be a great haven for reducing stress or it can add much of its own. In this section we start with a simple test that tells you how stressed you are. We point out the legitimacy of emotions – and how each person is entitled to feel the way they do. We examine some of the quick fixes that people tend to use for handling life's pressures – and caution you against them. Then, we discuss feelings such as tension, frustration and anger, and suggest practical ways of handling them in yourself and in your partner. Step-by-step methods of purging negative feelings, relaxing, and reducing stress are given to help you make yours a truly successful marriage.

▶ 13 ◀

CHAPTER

STRESS

Stress is part of life. The word stress is borrowed from physics: humans, it is assumed, are like metals that resist moderate force but lose their resiliency under greater pressure.[44] Hence, the term stress describes a reaction or response to excessive pressures of some sort. Events or conditions that cause stress are called stressors, and there are four classes of them.[45]

- *Acute, time-limited stressors*. A visit to a doctor, a close call while attempting to cross a street, or a bad illness are some examples.
- *Stressor sequences*. Divorce, loss of job, or death of a loved one are some instances.
- *Chronic, intermittent stressors*. Examples are periodic visits to a dentist, on and off lower back pain, or travel demands of the job.
- *Chronic stressors*. Severe and permanent illness, long-standing marital difficulties, or inability to overcome financial problems are some cases.

Psychologist Steven E. Hobfoll offers an explanation of stress based on the conservation of resources: "People strive to retain, protect, and build resources and what is threatening to them is the potential or actual loss of these valued resources."[44] This theory is supported by the facts and helps in day to day handling of stress.

A visit to a doctor and a close call while trying to cross a street are stressful incidents for good reasons. Both are threats to the person's well-being and involve potential pain or even death.

Divorce or death of a loved one – stressor sequences – are a loss of precious resources. A spouse is a great source of security, need-satisfaction, and love, which are vital resources of life.

Life is full of visits to dentists and difficult situations that recur regularly. They can certainly add up to a serious threat to our well-being. And of course, everyone is at risk of permanent problems related to health and other matters – chronic stressors.

In this context, one's well-being can be compared to a bank account. People work to build it and there are expenses to be drawn from it. If the income is greater than the expenditure, then the account is in fine shape. When demands exceed savings, then there is trouble – stress.

People do many things to build up their 'well-being' accounts. Following good health practices, exercising, working to save money for the rainy day ahead, establishing and maintaining good relationships with other people, and so on. All these activities add to a person's resources and reduce the impact of various stressors. However, we do very little to reduce psychological stresses – stresses of the mind – that result from just about everything in life, including relationships.

Relationships thrive on good feelings and take a beating from bad feelings; emotions and stress go hand in hand. A person who is stressed frequently transfers and transmits some of his or her stress to another. Regardless of whether or not you are married or planning to get married, you need to know about your own stress level in order to manage stress effectively. Are you stressed, and if so how badly? Get an idea by taking the following test.

TEST YOUR STRESS QUOTIENT

Here is a simple stress test. Give yourself a score for each question:

0 = Never
2 = Once in a while
4 = Often
6 = Always

	SCORE
1. Do you eat on the run?	____
2. Do you feel tired and run down?	____
3. Do you have sleeping problems?	____
4. Are you too tired to exercise?	____
5. Do you feel overwhelmed by various demands?	____
6. Do you drink, smoke, or eat more when tense?	____
7. Do you feel like wanting to get away from it all?	____
8. Do you worry about your weight?	____
9. Do you worry about your finances?	____
10. Do you worry about your health?	____
11. Do people get on your nerves?	____
12. Do you catch colds easily?	____
TOTAL SCORE	____

If your total score is:

0–16 = You don't show much sign of stress.
18–30 = There is room for improvement.
32–72 = You should start looking seriously for ways of reducing stress.

SETTING EXPECTATIONS

How we feel is importantly influenced by our expectations and whether or not they are realized. Unrealized expectations lead to disappointment, anger, depression and other stressful emotions. Realized expectations, on the other hand, make us feel good and bring us joy. Hence it is important that our expectations are realistic ones.

● *Set high, but attainable, goals for yourself.* Make allowances for the possibility that some of your goals may not materialize. Be kind to yourself. Give yourself credit for setting high goals – strive to reach them, but never consider falling short as failure. Remember the story of Thomas Edison. He was asked how he felt failing in more than 1400 experiments before succeeding in making the first incandescent light bulb. He responded, "Failing? I just showed 1400 ways of not making light bulbs."

● *Set lower expectations for other people.* By so doing you will not be terribly disappointed with others – you'll be genuinely pleased when they exceed what you expect. This doesn't mean that you have to tell everyone you really don't expect anything at all from them. This is something that you keep in the privacy of your own mind.

REDUCING FRUSTRATION

Frustration is a bad feeling and it is directly proportional to one's expectations and attachments. If you want to reduce your frustration, then cut back on them. This does not mean that you should renounce the world, withdraw into a monastery, and take the vow of poverty. It means that you remain in the world, very much involved and participating, yet become more detached from it. Avoid ascribing exaggerated importance to things – things that you own, that you don't own and wish that you did, and things that others own. Detachment demands the conquering of envy, too. The greater the envy, the higher the frustration and unhappiness.

There are many philosophical and cultural differences between the East and the West – both have something to teach each other. Eastern culture is known for its fatalistic view of life. In the West, this is sometimes called oriental fatalism – with derogatory connotations. It runs counter to the attitude prevalent in the West that one should take charge and make one's own fate.

We recommend aiming for the middle ground. We are firm believers in moderation in all things. It is healthy to do what you can to be in charge of your life. But this in-charge mentality should not make for rigidity – the inability to bend a little, to take your setbacks calmly. As the saying goes, what you can't cure, endure. A measure of acceptance is a wonderful means of not allowing you to get into a rage whenever things don't quite work out the way you expect them to.

A while ago, we came across a piece of advice that we would like to pass on to you – life is ten percent what you make it and 90 percent how you take it.

AVOIDING MENTAL OVERLOAD

Mental fatigue is as real as physical tiredness. Somehow people better accept, understand, and respect physical fatigue while allowing their minds to become exhausted. Mental fatigue comes from overwork and overload, and can lead to over-reacting, bad feeling and illness.

The overload comes from three different areas.

- *Sensory overload.* We are constantly bombarded by both wanted and unwanted stimulation – the noise of trains, buses, trucks, automobiles, planes, factories, the ever-present radio and television – even the stimulants in the coffee and tea we drink.

All these stimulants literally pollute and tire the brain. Studies have shown that working in a noisy environment is very stressful.[46] Why? Noise intrudes into your brain and keeps on working at it and tiring it. Some people voluntarily subject themselves to this overload by watching a great deal of television or going nowhere without their headphones. This is a form of addiction. The brain is conditioned to this stimulation and actively seeks it. Of course, like all addictions, it exacts a price.

- *Information overload.* We live in an age of information explosion. The drive to know is a powerful human motivator and there is so much to learn and to keep up with. There is a little Renaissance man in all of us; we try to gather, absorb, and assimilate information about everything. The result is that we haul around in our minds mounds of half-digested or undigested information. Soon there is a congestion, chaos, and trouble.

● *Emotional overload.* No man is an island any longer. We are all interconnected in so many ways, and our complex society exacts a heavy price from us. We have to deal with many people and situations in our own personal lives – how to handle the boss, how to avoid hurting feelings, how to keep on smiling when we really want to scream. Add to this all the stressful events we share in common – helplessly watching masses of emaciated famine victims on television, hearing news of death and destruction, learning about misfortunes of others.

To the mind, they all add up to the same thing – a heavy load to haul. Like an engine working at full throttle, wear and tear are inevitable.

Our advice for avoiding mental overload:

● Do what you can to reduce intrusive noise and the barrage of unwanted sensory assaults. For instance, don't listen to the radio or watch television too often. When you do, set the volume as low as possible.

● Use some of the quiet time you save to give your mind a break. All this intrusive stimulation is like having unwanted guests. Give the mind a chance to do some house-cleaning.

● Don't try to know everything about everything, or to save the world single-handedly. You can't do it anyway.

● Be sympathetic to the sufferings of others – understand their plight and see if there is something you can do to help. But avoid being empathetic in every instance – suffering vicariously in every misfortune. Indiscriminate empathy drains you, and when you are drained, you are of little good to anyone, including yourself.

COMMON MISHANDLING OF STRESS

We are not born with healthy skills for handling stress. We do what we can under duress and many of the things we do are quick fixes or the wrong moves.

● *Self-medicating.* Trying to put out the fire of anguish by drinking alcohol or taking mood-altering drugs is a widespread practice. People do this because it is a 'quick fix.' And quick fixes give temporary relief – a sort of time-out, a break from the raging battle. Studies show that abusive drinkers and alcoholics are 'escape' drinkers – they rely on alcohol to make their troubles go away or take them away from their troubles.[47]

● *Denying*. Attempting to soothe ourselves by turning a blind eye to something worrying or threatening us is another popular strategy. It is a form of 'easy fix.' An example is refusing to accept that one is in serious financial trouble – a sort of wishing the trouble away, as if saying, "If I don't see it, then it is not there."

● *Repressing*. We also hide some worries inside other worries – like suitcases within suitcases. They are there all right, but we are not consciously aware of them. For instance, we might deeply bury the thought that we are carriers of a genetic disease that may suddenly spring upon us.

● *Attributing*. Gathering all our negative emotions into a few manageable bundles gives a false sense of security – of knowing what or who are the culprits. For instance, we might blame all our unhappiness on our spouse for supposedly failing to live up to our expectations. Then, a natural tendency is to unload this burden – get divorced. And, to our astonishment, we find out that we did not unload the unhappiness along with the spouse.

● *Blurring*. Another strategy is to defuse a crisis by a 'leveling' process – letting worries just run riot, not denying them and not paying much attention to any of them. This frequently leads to a condition of general malaise and constant unhappiness. In this condition, we can identify some of the things that are bothering us, but just about everything looks equally formidable or equally unimportant.

● *Surrendering*. When we resign ourselves to the inevitability of our misfortunes and our hurts, then surrender is the chosen option. There is a difference between acceptance and surrender; acceptance is a sensible resolution to endure what cannot be changed, but surrender is a premature raising of the white flag. Sometimes, surrender may take the extreme form of suicide.

Our view is that opting for one or more of these unhealthy methods of handling stress is always seductive, and they should not even be considered until we have exhausted the numerous other healthful ways of handling frustration.

DANGER SIGNALS

Emotional or psychological illnesses are as real and common as physical illnesses, and just as destructive. They range from mild to deadly, from temporary to chronic; may have gradual or sudden onsets; and can be triggered by neurochemical as well as psychological causes. We can hardly deal with this topic in detail here, but we would like to point out some of the warning signals that are indicative of possible emotional problems. Once any of these signs is spotted, it is wise to see a psychiatrist, a therapist, or your family physician – without delay – for expert evaluation. It is prudent to be alert to these danger signals, but equally important is the realization that the diagnosis is best left to the experts. They are better qualified as well as more objective.

The presence of one or more of the following should alert us to the need to seek help: inexplicable fatigue; eating disturbances – such as loss of appetite or overeating; sleep disturbances – such as inability to fall asleep, interrupted sleep, recurring nightmares; uncontrollable crying spells; suicidal thoughts; loss of interest in matters such as personal grooming or social activities; inability to concentrate; frequent colds and infections; tension or inexplicable headaches; drinking alcohol excessively, alone, or in the mornings; resorting to illicit drug use or relying on mind-altering prescription drugs ; presence of high anxiety or panic attacks; being irritable and easily provoked.

Mental illness is now accorded the same legitimacy as physical illness, and people are beginning to listen to what mental health professionals say about disorders of the mind. The individual should feel no more guilt and shame than someone afflicted with any physical illness. Obviously, certain attitudes and practices increase the risk while others lower the likelihood for psychological illness, as is also the case for physical disorders. Hence, the need for 'hygiene' is not limited to physical hygiene. Much of this book is devoted to a mental hygiene that can significantly help a marriage as well as the individual's well-being.

▶ 14 ◀

CHAPTER

PEOPLE SKILLS

The human mind usually takes the easiest and the quickest path to a conclusion, and one result is that we accept simple answers even when they are plain wrong. In many instances we force our views on reality, trying to make it conform to our thinking – instead of the other way around. The tendency to jump to conclusions about people can make us feel bad too often and unnecessarily.

FORMING IMPRESSIONS

All kinds of people are extremely important in our lives. So sizing them up is as vital as watching our step in the dark. How do we form our impressions of people? We start with a quick scan, almost instantaneous and automatic. This gives us the first impression. In most cases, we won't go much beyond this first impression stage, since we encounter so many people all the time.

The instant we meet someone, we classify him or her as good or bad. This superficial assessment is appealing because of its economy and speed. We quickly adopt an appropriate posture toward each person we meet. The main problem is that once we label someone we tend to look for and find facts that support our initial appraisal, because it is a lot easier and more desirable to confirm our views than to change them.

By labeling people as bad, we begin feeling bad toward them. We ourselves end up as the victim of the negative feeling. We are the biggest losers when we dislike others, because every time we see or hear them, or think about them, the bad feelings take their toll.

By deciding too hastily that people are 'good' we may fare no better; we may be disappointed or get hurt. The best thing to do is to avoid giving people labels and jumping to conclusions. Make it very difficult for someone to earn a 'bad' label – not only in fairness to them, but also to make life easier on yourself.

PEOPLE AS STRESSORS

People are a major source of stress, even the people we dearly love – particularly the people we dearly love. Arguments between couples are by far the most distressing events in everyday life.[48]

The more people we deal with, the greater the total stress. We cannot avoid associating with certain people, such as members of our immediate family, or people at work. But beyond that it is important that we associate with people who do us more emotional good than harm. For instance, we shouldn't blindly belong to every group and organization that will take us, because any belonging exacts emotional and other costs. It is wise to do a bit of thinking and evaluating before getting involved. What will the demands be? What about the benefits? Can we afford the additional stress?

Anxieties, worries, and negative feelings come from all sources and in various sizes. Like ghosts, they dance about in our heads. Some we can recognize. They are terribly menacing and are on our minds constantly. But many are in the background, making their contributions to our unhappiness.

These negative feelings are burdens that we haul around. Strange things happen; these feelings interbreed, make new combinations, and multiply. That is why people may feel very anxious – almost panicky – yet not be able to pinpoint exactly what it is that is worrying them.

MOOD RECRUITMENT

The way we approach other people and handle our relationships is highly dependent on our temperament or habitual mood. A good mood begets a better mood while a bad mood begets a worse one. This happens by a recruitment process in the mind – one bad mood or memory activates other dormant ones and soon there is a storm of negative feelings engulfing us. Similarly, a pleasant thought or event activates other positive memories and enhances one's overall mood. This mood recruitment is rooted in the way the brain works. There are up to 100 billion nerve cells in the human brain. Some of these cells are dedicated to special functions, even before birth. For instance, some cells run the body's vital operations of circulation and digestion. Others receive their assignments in the first few years of life; yet others remain relatively unassigned during the course of one's life. Also, recent research shows that there is fierce competition among brain cells. Not all of them survive and not every one is included in the varied brain networks. It is likely that the more active a given brain system is, the more cells it will recruit. This greater cell inclusion, in turn, makes for a greater activity and dominance of the heavily recruited system.

It is not far-fetched, therefore, to believe that the temperamentally optimistic and the habitually pessimistic – or the sunny disposition versus the gloomy type – are reflecting the dominance of their different brain networks. And these brain networks can be selectively enhanced or suppressed by a variety of means – with greater ease on a short-term than a long-term basis, because the networks are deeply entrenched. Once the intervention ends, the tendency is for the hierarchy to revert back to its original state. Chemicals such as mood-enhancers, tranquilizers and alcohol are powerful means of disrupting the brain's prevailing equilibrium. Psychological events, such as stress, anxiety and disappointment are also powerful influences on the brain system. Some psychological influences may even be more important in reorganizing the brain system by virtue of their potency and/or severity. Both chemicals and psychological interventions produce their results by changing the chemistry and physiology of brain systems.

It is wise, therefore, to stack the odds in your favor. Make it a habit to look on the sunny side of life; to look for all your little blessings. By so doing, you are likely to improve your disposition significantly, and this will influence the people around you.

People do all kinds of things to escape negative states and to experience positive feelings. Overeating, or eating at special restaurants; buying expensive clothes; traveling to exotic and idyllic places; seeking exciting company; accumulating possessions; collecting rare items; abusing drugs and alcohol. Drugs are particularly relied upon for jump-starting – to move the person to a more desirable psychological state. In the age of instant gratification, quick fixes of all sorts are in great demand.

But other, more wholesome activities such as physical exercise, reading good books, prayer and meditation can be employed to make us feel good. Physical exercise, for example, may help us gain a sense of vitality, make us proud of the self-discipline we mustered, and even enhance the brain's production of 'high-inducing' endorphins. Reading good books can inspire confidence, give us insight, and place the problems of life in proper perspective. Prayers serve to connect us with a Supreme Creator and mitigate our unhappiness. Meditation gives us serenity and the feeling of well-being that comes with it.

VENTING VS. DUMPING

There is a big difference between venting and dumping. Venting is at the heart of a good marriage. That's why you have a spouse, a partner, a true friend to help you get rid of your emotional hurts, anxieties and worries – and aid you in feeling better. So you can and should tell your spouse – your best friend – about what is bothering you. Sharing troubles with your partner is like each of you having a resident psychotherapist; a psychotherapist who is not expert in the art and science of therapy, but is a willing listener and comforter. Hence, when you have a hard day at work – an argument with a co-worker, or an inconsiderate client – you can depend on your spouse to allow you to express your hurts and frustrations. When done properly, this sort of sharing is like dressing a wound; like physical ones, the wounds of the mind can also fester if left untended.

Dumping, on the other hand, is abuse of the privilege of venting. And it can take many forms. The difference between venting and dumping is in the outcome; if by sharing your feelings you end up feeling better without making your spouse feel bad, then it is venting. If you end up feeling better and the spouse ends up feeling bad, that's dumping. We cannot give you a comprehensive formula to use – you have to develop the skill. A good practice is to avoid overdoing it, as if you were running to 'mother' or 'dad' with your slightest hurts. Also, good timing is important: don't do it when the both of you are on edge. Finally, do a little 'packaging' of the delivery to soften the blow on your partner. Start gently and you, yourself, participate in the dressing of the wound. It is definitely a case of dumping when you hand over your problem and make it your spouse's.

Our advice is to look after your emotional well-being. And a good way to do that is to reduce the influence of other people in making you feel bad. When they succeed in making you feel bad, get out of that negative mood state rapidly. The longer you stay in the emotional pit, the heavier its toll on you. By the same token, try not to hurt other people's feelings – particularly your spouse's. Humans have a powerful disposition toward reciprocity; if you affect someone's feelings either positively or negatively, they will feel compelled to reciprocate in kind.

▶ 15 ◀

CHAPTER

PURGING BAD FEELINGS

Think of the mind as a pond with all kinds of things in it – some floating on top, others somewhere in the middle, and yet others way down deep. Worries and anxieties roam around the pond of the mind, take up room, create confusion, and make us unhappy – while our blessings drift in the background. As time goes on, more and more trouble-makers pile up and breed. The pond of the mind needs regular cleaning – we need to trap the trouble-makers and ship them out while keeping the good items and giving them the prominence they deserve. Here is a way of doing just that.

● Organize a notebook for yourself. Divide each page in two by drawing a line right down the middle. Mark the left side good and the right side bad.

● On the good side, with a pen, write all the blessings and joys of your life. Be thorough, take your time, and don't miss anything – large or small.

● On the bad side write, in pencil, every item that is troubling you. Don't miss anything. All troubles fall into one of three categories. Decide if each is 1) baseless or unimportant, 2) solvable, or 3) unsolvable.

● First, take your eraser to the problems you have tagged as baseless and unimportant. As you erase each one on the paper, picture it as vividly as you can in your mind and watch it vanishing from your consciousness. Some of these problem thoughts will come back, like homing pigeons, but you capture and banish them again on your next inventory-taking. Eventually, they give up and stay out.

● Next, take each solvable problem and develop a sensible solution for it. Keep working at it and whittle it down. As it begins to yield, run your eraser over it to make it fade until you completely get rid of it and erase it altogether.

● Then, tackle the problems you have tagged as unsolvable. Make sure that they are indeed hopeless – at least for the foreseeable future. Strip each problem of all the unnecessary importance that it had acquired, and then accept it for what it is. This acceptance in itself clears the air and brings invaluable relief.

Here are some examples of the three classes of problems that roam the mind.

● *Worrying about impressing everyone*. This is an instance of the unimportant. Of course it is nice to make good impressions, but worrying about it is too heavy a price to pay. Chances are that you'll make better impressions by not being so obsessed about it. So list it, erase it thoroughly and toss it out – it is wasting precious effort.

● *Being unhappy with your job*. This is a case of a solvable problem. Do some serious thinking. Talk with your spouse, job counselors, potential employers. Explore all kinds of possibilities. Be creative and generate a number of options. In most instances a viable solution is awaiting you.

● *Having a physical handicap*. Being blind, to take a powerful example, is an unsolvable problem, but not the end of the world. No amount of worrying and resentment is going to do a bit of good. Take it for what it is, the loss of something precious. But there are so many other blessings in life, and one shouldn't let even this problem exact too great a price. Once blind, you can't get your sight back, but you can surely do a lot with all the other gifts that you still have – you still have your inner vision, no less valuable than your eyes.

Don't forget to work on the good side of the notebook. Be creative. Read each item and ponder about it time and again. Rewrite your list in larger letters with colored pens and decorate it if you like. Give your blessings more prominence and room in your mind – let them breed with other good things and expand. The more you ponder these positive items, the less time is left for the negative ones.

Every time you work on the bad side, treat yourself by going over the good side. It gives you the strength you need and it makes you feel more content.

USING MENTAL IMAGERY

It is said that life is what you imagine it to be; that we live in the mind – a home we never leave. So the condition of this home that we live in is critical to the quality of life. Using imagery, you can decorate this house, ventilate it with fresh air, and keep it warm and comforting. Here are some practical suggestions.

- *Use imagery to reduce stress.* To do this, focus on soothing images with closed eyes in a quiet place – away from the telephone, the television, the radio and other distractions.

For example, imagine yourself viewing the sunset on a body of water, with scattered clouds on the horizon. The rays of the sun, filtering through the clouds, are painting a magnificent panorama. Just let go of every thought and focus your whole attention on becoming part of the unfolding serenity.

Or imagine a night in the country with a full moon. A deep blanket of fresh snow covers the land, mountains stand majestically in the background, and silence envelops the whole scene in peaceful beauty. This form of imagery helps break the stranglehold of piled-up negative emotions.

- *Use imagery to expand your vision.* Before you can do something, you have to conceive it to be possible. An architect cannot just throw a bunch of building materials together and expect a magnificent edifice. It all starts with a conception, an idea, a vision of something exquisite. You are the architect of your life. So use your imagination to create a vision of the fulfilling and serene life you can have. Decorate the home of the mind in just the way you want it. Don't let it be cluttered by all kinds of pieces that don't belong.

EXERCISE

Exercise is not only good for the body, it is a balm to the mind. It is an excellent means of getting much pent-up tension out of the system. Of course, exercise is exertion – something we all tend to avoid.

People come up with all kinds of excuses for not exercising regularly. For example, they are dead tired after having done all the things that they have to do; or they just don't have the time. Exercise is not a luxury. It is a necessity for keeping us fit, in mind as well as body.

When it come to exercise, our advice is:

- do it;
- choose the form of exercise that you enjoy; but
- do it.

RELAXATION

Everyone wants to relax. But in a publication of the United States Department of Health and Human Services on relaxation[49] the opening sentence reads: "It is surprising how little Americans know about the art of relaxation." This is not just an American deficiency – it is worldwide. Relaxation is not only getting away from the tense daily grind, or simply the absence of stress. Relaxation generates satisfying feelings that create peace of mind.

> The continuing pressures of everyday life take a heavy toll on the physical and mental well-being of millions of people each year. Medical research into the origins of common diseases such as high blood pressure, heart

> disease, ulcers, and headaches show a connection between stress and the development of such ailments. In the area of mental health, stress frequently underlies emotional and behavioral problems, including nervous breakdowns. Various environmental factors – from noise and air pollution to economic disruptions, such as unemployment, inflation, and recession – can make living conditions even more stressful.[43]

It is commonplace for people to become so preoccupied with their day-to-day chores that they neglect their needs for relaxation. Or they seek to relax by certain activities that may cost them dearly, such as having a few drinks to unwind.[47] In urban industrial societies, many people become so accustomed to the idea of being productive that even their vacations become practices in exhaustion – through attempts at making them packed with things to do, learn, and experience.

> Far too few people know how to turn off their body clocks and gain satisfaction out of just being instead of always striving. The secret in getting the best results from attempts at relaxation is simple: Find those activities which give you pleasure, and, when you pursue them, commit your energies to total mental and physical well-being. If your diversion results in an artistic product, musical skills, further education, a better physique, or whatever, that's great. But remember that relaxation, not achievement is your main reason for participating in the activity.[43]

There are many healthy ways of relaxing. You should explore a number of them and choose several for yourself. For instance, you may find jogging relaxing. That's great, but you should also try other things as well – such as self-relaxation. One form of self-relaxation involves stretching on the floor, flat on your back, placing a rolled bath-towel under the small of your back. While in this stretched position, close your eyes and systematically tense and relax each muscle group in your body.

Toward the end of this exercise, imagine that all the tension is draining away from your head, down your torso, along your legs, and out of your toes.

This kind of relaxation is particularly soothing at the end of a long, tense day at work. In deciding what to do for relaxation, keep three rules in mind.

- Don't be afraid of choosing something new and different. Have an open mind – be adventurous.
- Make sure that you enjoy the activity you choose and that it is relaxing. Don't make it another mountain to climb.
- Accept relaxation as a legitimate need that must be met on a regular basis – daily, or more often. You shouldn't wait until you are overwhelmed to think of doing some relaxing.

PRAYER

Praying involves your relationship with the Creator – but it also makes you feel good. Prayer can be a powerful means of relaxation, reassurance, and relieving tension. Praying frees you from the trap of your immediate pains. It works like a reverse microscope – reducing seemingly insurmountable problems down to size. The revealed religions of the world have a treasury of magnificent prayers, each suited to a particular state of mind.

Those who believe in a loving, caring, and ever-listening Creator may pray for His help or guidance. Others who do not believe in God can still pray to good effect. The words are balm to the wounds of the mind and the soul. There can be no harm in praying.

MEDITATION

In our book, *Creating a Successful Family*, we wrote:

> Meditation can be a marvelous tool for enhancing the well-being of the individual. Meditation is not limited to only one particular, highly ritualized method. On the contrary, it should be a personalized practice to yield its benefits, and it should be in the style that suits you best.

> Meditation is taking time out of the day to create a mental stillness that can rest the mind. An interval of quiet serenity, it is an occasion for self-reconstitution, an opportunity to relax, reduce tension, and feel good. It is a means of sorting things out, promoting mental health, and cleaning the dross of daily life from the mind. It allows for a break from the routine and a reconnection with the inner being, providing an opportunity to get to know yourself better. Meditation is also a key to the development of insight.[28]

There are many good books on meditation. We recommend that you read a few of them and try some of the procedures that appeal to you. You should also consider designing your own way of meditating. You can customize it to best meet your own needs.

Some people use several methods of meditation, not just one. For instance, when your head is buzzing with the overload of a day's bombardment, you may want to put a stop to it and create mental silence by meditating. One way to do this is to sit yourself down comfortably, breathe rhythmically, and count from one to five with each breath – at all times focusing only on counting your breath. Continue this practice for a few minutes and the relentless buzzing in your head comes to a halt.

For many people, meditation works better than drugs, alcohol, and the psychotherapist's couch combined, in relieving tension and creating relaxation – at no cost, except a touch of faith, a bit of effort, and a little time. You and your spouse may want to try praying and meditating together. For some couples, this togetherness serves as another occasion for shared relaxation with added synergy.

STRESS REDUCTION

There are numerous excellent books on the theory and practices of relaxation and the reduction of stress.[50] The following procedure is a modified version of the technique originally proposed by Benson. For more details see his book.[51]

It is inspired by meditation practices of eastern culture, and has four essential elements: a quiet environment; a mental device such as a word or a phrase to be repeated in a specific manner; a passive attitude; and a comfortable position.

- A *quiet environment*. A calm and quiet setting, with as few distractions as possible, is best. Keep intrusions such as the telephone and the television out.
- A *mental device*. Choose a device – a word or a phrase with positive connotations – to help you concentrate. Repeat the word or the phrase.
- A *passive attitude*. Assume a passive attitude and don't worry about how you are doing. Let go and let things just happen. When your mind wanders to other thoughts, abandon them and go back to repetition of the mental device. The key is to make less effort, rather than simply adding the demand to relax. Relaxation will follow if you let go.
- A *comfortable position*. Position yourself comfortably to reduce muscle tension, but not to the point of falling asleep. You may sit in a cross-legged position, if you like.

The following is a suggested procedure for reducing your stress to a more tolerable level:

- Sit comfortably in a quiet place.
- Keep your eyes closed, to minimize distractions.
- Start relaxing your muscles, beginning at your feet and advancing toward your face.
- Breathe gently and rhythmically. Become aware of your breathing.
- Repeat your mental device – a word or a short phrase – every time you breath out.
- Spend ten to twenty minutes, twice a day if possible, using this procedure. You may open your eyes to check the time, but avoid alarm clocks and other gadgets that signal time.
- You will achieve greater and greater relaxation as you continue this practice.

▶16◀

CHAPTER

DEALING WITH EMOTIONS

To feel emotions deeply is to be human. When we feel good, life is a joy; when we feel bad, it is a burden. You need to know how to deal with feelings – to express them and make them work for both you and your spouse. "Seeing is believing, but feeling is the truth," says Thomas Fuller. Also, Eleanor Roosevelt was correct in saying, "No one can make you feel inferior without your consent." Feeling inferior is one form of feeling bad. Your consent is also required for all the other negative or positive feelings.

EXPRESSING FEELINGS

Being a considerate, kind, and controlled person does not mean that you should not express your feelings. On the contrary, it is important that you do. For instance, if your spouse says or does something that hurts your feelings, you should let it be known.

● *It is not healthy to bottle up one's hurts.* Keeping things inside can create a sort of psychological time bomb that can go off unexpectedly. "A riot is at the bottom of the language of the unheard," Martin Luther King, Jr. observed. Studies show that spouses seem to think that their stresses and concerns are obvious to their partners when this is not the case.[52] Also, stress and hurt feelings are the main causes of numerous bodily illnesses and contributory to many more.[53] So you must find healthy ways of emptying your cup. One way to do that is to tell your spouse how you feel – as clearly, yet as gently as you can.

● *Misunderstanding can be the real culprit.* Your partner may not have the slightest clue that what she or he is doing is hurtful to you. Clamming up and feeling angry inside is not smart. When you express your feelings – and you should – try hard not to make your spouse the target of your outburst. Direct your feelings against the hurtful words and actions, and not against your partner. Of course it is hard to separate the *actor* from the *action*. But you love the actor and you dislike the action. So make an effort to keep the one you love and banish the other.

For example, your wife may say, "Oh, you have such nice long hair, those locks – most girls would give their right arm to have them." You see a little grin on her face and you sense some teasing and perhaps an allusion to femininity. Whether she is just teasing you or meaning to imply that you look feminine with that long hair is irrelevant. The fact is that you see it as an attack on your masculinity. So don't let that pass, and don't bottle up that hurt.

Express your feelings. Clear the air by saying something like this, "Well, do you really like my hair this way? You don't think I look feminine, do you? I couldn't be very feminine if I love a wonderful woman like you. But if you really think I look silly, I'll think about getting a short haircut."

She may surprise you by saying, "Oh, no, honey, I just love it the way it is. I was just admiring your beautiful head of hair." By expressing yourself you cleared the air, proved your hunch completely wrong, and instead of feeling bad about her you got closer to her.

If she had meant to tease you about your hair and replied, "Well, honey, it is a little too long" – you also learned something. Then, depending on how you feel about what she said, you can take it from there. You might say, "I really love it the way it is and I hope that you get to like it too and won't tease me about it. As for what people might think, let them think whatever they want. I can't change that."

On all the occasions when you have an emotional encounter, the cardinal rule is to address the problem not the person, if you value the relationship. Always use 'I' messages. For instance, if your husband fails to do something that he had promised to do, you can say, "I feel let down," instead of "you didn't keep your word." Expressing yourself in this way is preferable. You express your feelings and let him know of your disappointment, without directly attacking him. He may make amends. Further, he cannot argue about how you feel. You feel let down – that's how you feel, and feelings are not really debatable and arguable. Each of us is entitled to feel the way we do, as irrational as it may seem to others.

UNDERSTANDING FRUSTRATION AND ANGER

We get frustrated when we can't have the things we want or get our own way. Also, we become frustrated when things that we don't want happen to us. But frustrations are part of everyday life. People come up with all sorts of ways of dealing with their frustrations. Sometimes we use ingenious solutions, and at other times we do all kinds of not very smart things.

For instance, if the automobile you are driving veers off the road in dense fog and you find yourself in a ditch instead of at the very important meeting you were headed for – frustration and anger are the likely outcome. How do you take this situation? You can try and laugh, be a little detached – not exactly everyone's likely reaction. Or you do what most people tend to do – furiously step on the gas to work their way out of the ditch while the spinning wheels are sinking the car deeper and deeper in the mud. Obviously a few choice words and banging of the fist on various parts of the car are also in order! Alternatively, you could reason with yourself that a towing service is needed, call for assistance, and catch a cab to your appointment.

Take the case of the little toddler who wants to run in the field like the older children, but can't keep up with them. She stumbles, falls, gets farther behind, and screams in rage. The parents may attribute her screaming to the pain of falling down. Yet it could be just as much the psychological pain of wanting something and not being able to have it – in this case, keeping pace with the older children.

We all, young and old, have a capacity for stress, anger, frustration, and all the other psychological pains. We bottle up these burdens, but we cannot store these hurts indefinitely. Each of us has to find healthy ways of regularly emptying our personal cup. Otherwise it will overflow and cause a lot of damage.

When your cup gets filled at work and you haven't learned a harmless way of emptying it, the victim of your tensions and frustrations may be a loved one at home. The slightest provocation is all that's needed for you to explode. It is imperative that the cup be emptied; unless you find healthy ways of regularly draining it, it will drain you.

COMMON REACTIONS TO FRUSTRATION

Frustration is energizing; it is an impetus to action. A powerful tendency is to use force, which may lead to physical violence, as in the case of a frustrated child who pushes another to grab a toy. The child's behavior is one form of aggression. Other forms are more subtle but just as destructive. It is important that they are recognized and avoided. When frustration leads to anger, one may become the target of one's own wrath.

● *Aggression against the self*. This is probably the most widely practiced form of aggression, and most people don't even realize it. It involves making the self the target of anger, as the nearest and safest outlet for one's wrath. Further, rightly or wrongly, we often tend to blame ourselves for our failures, hurts and frustrations. This may involve:

> *Self-deprecation* – pouring verbal abuse on oneself. In a fit of anger, calling oneself names such as 'idiot,' 'worthless,' 'fool.' We learn to be abusive toward ourselves from others. Siblings, adults and even parents

are the teachers. They point out how dumb we are when we make mistakes, how unworthy we are when we don't measure up, and punish us when we are in violation of their expectations.

Self-beating and injury – physically hurting oneself. It may involve hitting, mutilation, and even suicide.

Self-induced illness – keeping the tension of anger inside us causes actual physical illnesses of various sorts, such as ulcers, forms of high blood pressure, asthma, skin rashes, and eating disorders.

● *Aggression against others.* When anger is channeled out toward others, it may take one or more of several forms of violence.

Passive. The main feature here is the failure of normal responses. This may take endless forms. For instance, you may refuse to speak to him or act coolly toward him. He may neglect doing certain chores. Harm is inflicted by not doing things.

Verbal. This is the most pervasive form of violence – verbal abuse, both subtle and blatant. It is also potentially the most devastating. Verbal violence can take numerous forms: being abusive to one's face, saying things behind one's back, spreading rumor and innuendo are some examples. Verbal violence is a deadly sin, particularly in marriage.

Hostile. In this instance, just inflicting harm is the goal itself. This is sadistic behavior – an indication of serious psychological problems. Throwing rocks at animals, just to hurt them; scaring people by reckless driving; and simply being obnoxious toward other people are examples.

Instrumental. This form of aggression is practiced with the aim of accomplishing something. Spanking a child in the hope of correcting misbehavior, mugging someone for their money, pushing your spouse to make him do what you want and so forth.

Displaced. When a safe target or an innocent party is the focus of our wrath we have a case of displaced violence. Having a rough day at work and pouring out our anger against a loved one is an example.

Social. Making society as a whole the victim is a common form of violence. Intentionally littering, violating traffic laws, defacing and damaging public property, and persecuting or assaulting total strangers are some examples.

Environmental. Some people get a perverse sense of satisfaction out of doing things that damage the environment. This is an indirect way of trying to get back at one's real source of frustration.

Group. Group aggression is the banding together of several people against a target, such as the father and the daughter turning on the mother, the in-laws joining forces against the son-in-law, mobs attacking one person.

Socially-condoned. Some forms of violence are promoted by society. Brutality in many sports such as boxing, and the military culture that culminates in nations going to war, are some examples.

FRUSTRATION LEADING TO OTHER BEHAVIOR

Frustration just about always produces anger but it doesn't necessarily lead to aggression and violence. Frustration can also serve a constructive function, such as spurring the invention of work-saving devices.

Most people, however, either don't know how or don't want to make the effort of dealing with their frustrations constructively, and think that frustration and anger can be mollified by cheap short-cut strategies. They seem cheap because they are just that – cheap in the sense of requiring little effort and delivering even less in the way of results. Here are some of the widely used cheap ways.

- *Fantasy.* If things out there are not to our liking, we simply make them so by fantasizing. In our fantasy world we tell off the boss, live in a palace, pay the bills, and so on. Trouble is that no amount of fantasizing changes very much. Further, excessive fantasizing takes precious time that could be devoted to doing something about the source of our frustration. As we spend more and more time in this make-believe world, chances are that other problems keep piling up.

● *Apathy*. Adopting the devil-may-care attitude – apathy – is particularly likely when someone is faced with a long-standing, severe, and hopelessly frustrating situation. But there are very few situations in life that are totally hopeless. There are always ways of eliminating, or at least reducing, frustration.

● *Chemicals*. Alcohol and drugs are used to relieve and numb the mind. These are short-cuts that bring temporary relief, usually at a high cost.

● *Treats*. All kinds of self-indulgences may be triggered by frustration and anger. These negative emotions make us feel bad, and a central goal of our lives is to feel good. Hence, when we feel bad, we may try to cancel that by doing things that make us feel good. Overeating, excessive sleeping, sexual promiscuity, and reckless spending are just a few examples.

What makes people even bother with destructive ways of handling their emotions? There are at least three reasons.

● *They are easier to learn and do*. Eating – particularly desserts – feels good. Buying and wearing expensive clothes may make one look better, attracts admiration and helps soothe the hurts. These things are easy to do and require no skills.

● *They are quick fixes*. Relief is only a swallow away, drug commercials promise – capitalizing on the powerful attraction of quick fixes. Consuming alcohol, taking drugs, and many other activities have this desirable feature.

● *They are natural*, in the sense of being crude and primitive. We acquire many of these bad habits early in life when no one bothers to teach us more difficult, but healthier, techniques. When a child is angered, his first impulse is to scream, push and even say a few choice words. It is through the process of humanization that he gradually learns more appropriate ways of dealing with his emotions. Yet some of these early behaviors become so firmly established that they may stay with him – sometimes in disguised forms – for the rest of his life.

But not everything that is easy, gives quick results and seems natural is necessarily the right thing. There are some excellent ways of handling frustration and anger and still feeling good.

GATHERING ANXIETIES

It is distressing to have all kinds of bad feelings, worries and anxieties roaming freely in our minds. The matter becomes even worse when many of these undesirables cannot be properly identified or traced. A common practice is to try to tag and capture them. So we cast a psychological net and try to identify as many of these floaters as we can in the hope of discovering how they can best be dealt with. Much of psychotherapy is an attempt at helping a person to identify anxieties, worries, and fears in the hope of getting rid of them.

One common tendency is to collect many of these negative feelings and ascribe them to someone or something. For instance, "He is the one who makes me anxious. He never seems to be satisfied with what I do. I feel so tense with him. Yeah, that's it. He makes me anxious." Or one may gather the anxieties and project them onto one's job, "Boy, they sure put a lot of pressure on me. Lousy pay and long hours and all those demands." In a sense, this is the practice of blaming others. No one, not even God, is exempt from becoming the object of blame. The trouble is that, more often than not, divorcing the spouse, quitting the job, and renouncing God will do little to eliminate the projected anxieties.

LEARNED HELPLESSNESS

Learned helplessness is a belief that we are helpless in controlling things – the idea that what we do is not causally related to the outcome of things.[54] There are many negative consequences to learned helplessness – a form of depression is one. A lot of learning takes place in marriage. The couple should inoculate itself against learned helplessness – this psychological disease of the modern age – by empowering each other whenever possible. Being able to influence outcomes, succeeding, developing confidence, and gaining approval are inoculations against learned helplessness – a disease of despair seen in many relationships.

▶ 17 ◀

CHAPTER

HANDLING YOUR PARTNER'S EMOTIONS

Any relationship falls into one of three categories: friendly–supportive, neutral–indifferent, or hostile–adversarial.[55] In this age of endless anxiety, frustration, and stress, helping your spouse handle these emotions is a key to having a friendly–supportive relationship. Remember that sharing good times as well as enduring bad times together cements the bond. The key word is *togetherness*. The way you maintain this togetherness is by empathy – feeling your partner's feeling – understanding, and love. From time to time, you must be ready to take that difficult mental trip to share his or her difficult feelings and lend your vital energies to hoist your partner, ever so gently, out of the dungeon.

Couples often do the exact opposite by inflicting additional pain during those agonizing times. The reason is partly the natural tendency to react – to react with the same mood and manner as the person we are dealing with. Here is an example. You come home upset because of an incident at work. The facts of the incident are not terribly relevant at this point – what is important is that you are angry and hurt.

What should your spouse do? Sit you down, interrogate you and prove to you that you blew a fuse unnecessarily? Or give you a hug, offer you a backrub, and just patiently listen to you let off steam? The first approach will deal a blow to the relationship, no matter how justified it is. No one appreciates being dressed down – particularly at moments like this, and by the person whose primary function is to love and comfort.

The opposite strategy – coming to your spouse's aid – results in increased affection. The time for reflecting on the facts of the situation and taking some corrective measures is after the hurt is soothed and with a clear head. Otherwise, crisis is added to crisis. And people are unfortunately at their worst – intellectually and emotionally – in crisis situations.

So don't tell her, "You should see some of the things that happen to me at work that I never tell you about. I guess you have a long way to go in learning the ways of the working world and not to lose your cool so easily." This practice is patronizing and amounts to psychological abandonment. When we need emotional support and we don't get it from our main source – the spouse – then we are literally abandoned. If our partner adds lecturing, interrogation and reprimand, then the pain is multiplied. Abandonment has to do with feelings and emotions, not facts or the question of right and wrong.

Further, by trying to prove the folly of your spouse's anger you are putting yourself in an adversarial position. No one would like this. Automatically, you will become associated with some of the negative features of the situation or the person that made her angry. This is an established fact of classical conditioning.[56]

When your spouse is angry or upset, our advice is:

- *Don't lose your own calmness*. This is not the time for you to start spouting. This is your turn to be the soother, the comforter and the one who cares.
- *Don't side with the 'enemy' or the source of hurt, no matter how tempting it may be*. The alliance of the couple demands that you don't take side against your spouse.
- *Don't lecture*. The emotional upheaval is hurtful enough. Let your partner tell you what he or she wants to, and

ventilate the hurt in your safe and caring presence. Resist the temptation to lecture and point out faults or flaws.

• *Scrutinize the facts, after the storm subsides.* Only after a large dose of comfort has soothed the hurt, may the two of you want to consult about the problem with clear heads and see if you can't help each other in avoiding such episodes in the future. It is preferable that the hurt party wants to do this. The other partner should not press for it, because the hurt person may not be in a mood for reliving the painful experience.

L.O.V.E. AND EMOTION

A good formula for handling your spouse's emotions is L.O.V.E.

- L = *Listen.* Listen with your all, patiently, and do very little talking yourself.
- O = *Observe.* Observe subtle clues, things that are not said, feelings, body language, and needs of the moment.
- V = *Value.* Respect the feelings, the disappointments and the hurts.
- E = *Empathize.* Feel with him or her. Share in the emotions just the same way as you would share your moments of joy together.

As you can see, this formula has no provisions for interrogating, patronizing, and lecturing.

GENERATING GOOD FEELINGS

Human beings react – and they usually react in kind. So if you want her to be nice to you, act nicely toward her. Nastiness and unkindness will most likely earn you the same. Marriage brings together two equal people into an intimate relationship. The term 'significant other,' which refers to one's mate, married or not, is highly descriptive. For most adults, the spouse is the most important person in their lives. And the more important the person is to you, the more strongly you react to him or her.

Couples travel in tandem in psychological space as they do in the physical world. When one spouse is in a bad mood, the other is likely to feel bad too. The challenge is for one of the pair to take the initiative, on any one occasion, and gently chart their course out of the emotional pit.

● *Retaliation and vengeance*. When people are hurt, they have a powerful tendency to retaliate and take revenge. Since there is so much interaction in marriage, there are unlimited opportunities for getting into this vicious cycle of retaliation and vengeance. For the most part, we don't even need to give it a lot of thought, or be consciously crafty, when we retaliate. It can happen so easily that it takes a serious effort to guard against retaliation. Retaliation is deadly to a friendly–supportive relationship – the foundation of a successful marriage. When one acts badly toward the other, the other tends to retaliate in kind and the atmosphere becomes poisonous. If there are more negative interactions than positive ones the marriage will become a torture.

When, on the other hand, the exchanges between the pair are positive and supporting, the marriage becomes a true haven worthy of any sacrifice. This type of marriage is successful enough to ride over occasional rough spots in its path.

● *Reciprocation*, returning kindness with usually greater kindness, is also a universal human trait.[57] Small favors often result in much greater paybacks. Avoid, so far as possible, saying or doing anything that would hurt the other. Instead, do and say things that will please – they trigger reciprocity. Then your marriage will be on a spiral of feeding on the energy of good feelings.

ORDINARY CONVERSATION

Ordinary conversation – talking at the dinner table, in the car, on walks, while watching television, and so on – can strengthen the bond or undermine the relationship. Much talking takes place between a couple – at least, it should. These seemingly unimportant and trivial talks are a good gauge of the condition of the marriage. If these conversations are up-beat, loving, and humorous, then the marriage is most likely in good shape. Talks not only reflect the present condition of the relationship, they also chart its future.

A sure sign of a bad marriage is when the couple don't talk much to each other. The silence may mean either:

- talking to each other has come to a dead stop, because the couple have very little in common; or
- every time they talk, the experience is negative. They get into an argument, they are on different wavelengths, or they simply bore each other.

The quality of the conversation influences the desire to spend time together. If every time you talk there is an argument or bad feeling, gradually you drift apart. If you want a successful marriage then you have to talk, joke, and banter. You have to explore emotions and let off steam. Let the worries of daily life go up in the hot air of verbal outflows.

You don't need to carry on the most sophisticated and deep conversation to meet this need. Be yourselves and relax. Your verbal nurturance can be serious, affectionate, reassuring – or as silly as both of you care to have it.

Talking is like air for marriage. No marriage can do without it. The couple produces the air, which may be just hot air, polluted, or as fresh as a gentle ocean breeze. Where there is no talking, there is no breathing. Talking, when positive, is also like glue. Without it the pair will drift apart, and each may find others to talk to – and possibly seek divorce in search of oxygen-bearing air elsewhere.

You should not overdo it – lots of fresh air is good, but don't make it a chilling draft. Don't wear out each other's ears just to keep talking; remember also that silence is golden. But it doesn't have to be a case of either/or. Marriage is full of paradoxes, and a successful marriage makes the paradoxes work for it. You should enjoy serene silence, ordinary talk, and intimate chats, as well as animated conversation. It takes work to find the track to success and it takes effort to stay on track.

What is the nature of your ordinary conversations? Are they mostly positive or negative? Take a couple of minutes and respond candidly to the following questionnaire. Make photocopies of the questionnaire for yourself and your spouse. Each of you should work the checklist in private, without the other being present or consulted. Later, it would be useful to compare your responses and see how closely you agree or disagree. This comparison may be very revealing. It may show that the both of you are in perfect agreement regarding your ordinary talking or that you have glaring differences of opinion. You can use the results to work on improving your conversation.

CONVERSATION QUALITY QUESTIONNAIRE

Think about all the times that the two of you are together and what characterizes your talks. Circle the alternative that best describes your conversation. Our conversations are:

	Never	Rarely	Often	Always
Fun	−3	−1	+2	+3
Sarcastic	+3	+1	−2	−3
Encouraging	−3	−1	+2	+3
About money problems	+3	+1	−2	−3
Romantic or poetic	−3	−1	+2	+3
Humorous	−3	−1	+2	+3
Stimulating	−3	−1	+2	+3
Argumentative	+3	+1	−2	−3
Positive	−3	−1	+2	+3
Loving	−3	−1	+2	+3
Critical of each other	+3	+1	−2	−3
Critical of other people	+3	+1	−2	−3
Educative	−3	−1	+2	+3
Considerate	−3	−1	+2	+3
One-sided monologues	+3	+1	−2	−3

Add together your positive scores and subtract the total of your negative scores to obtain your Conversation Quotient:

- 45 – you are perfect and your marriage is truly made in heaven. More likely though, you faked it!
- 35 or higher – you have an outstanding relationship – a truly exceptional one.

- 25–34 – you have a good relationship, but it has room for improvement.
- 10–24 – your relationship is rocky and not as satisfying as it should be. You have your work cut out for you.
- 9 or lower – the relationship is in need of immediate extra attention. Get to work right away.

PART five

MANAGING MARRIAGE

Marriage doesn't run itself. It is the couple's most important investment and it needs to be managed. Problems arise regularly. Challenges attempt to tear the union apart – as part of the universal force that aims to reduce every complex entity to its simplest elements. There will be disagreements and conflicts between the pair, in the individual life of each, and in their joint interaction with the outside world. All these events strain the marriage and sometimes even break it. In this section we discuss some of these concerns and present the marvelous all-purpose tool of consultation for dealing with challenges that confront couples. We detail the procedures, outline the steps and discuss the attitudes that make consultation work. We also examine other concerns – such as finances – and give advice on how to manage them effectively.

▶ 18 ◀

CHAPTER

SOLVING PROBLEMS

Living is the process of solving problems. Some problems may seem insoluble, but none are beyond partial solution; perfect solutions are not the only recourse. In many instances, partial solutions may mean the difference between a contented life and a defeated one. Learning to accept and live with a problem is in itself a form of solution. When you live alone, the problems are mainly yours and the solutions are up to you. In marriage all problems are joint problems and demand joint solutions.

To solve problems, you need to use your head, and everyone knows that two heads are better than one. What people don't know is that two heads are better than two: there is a synergy when two heads draw from their different stores of knowledge and experience to solve a problem together.

WHAT IS A 'PROBLEM'?

A problem is any difficulty or challenge that demands a solution. How do we know that we have a problem? We think about something and we conclude that we have a problem. Just as easily we can think about it and conclude that we don't have a problem. So if our thinking is conditioned to look for problems, we end up with mounds of them. If our thinking is programmed the other way, we end up with fewer problems.

Of course there are real problems, irrespective of our thinking style, but even these real problems expand and shrink in size depending on our thinking habits. Our thinking, therefore, is at the core of every problem. Hence, one of the most pressing problems is the way we think – adjusting and fine-tuning it is of the highest priority.

THINKING AND PROBLEM-SOLVING

Thinking is at the core of making decisions, choosing alternatives, and electing a course of action. Victor Frankl, a Viennese psychiatrist, comments, "During no moment of his life does man escape the mandate to choose among possibilities."[58] American psychologist Abraham Maslow proposed that mental patients are not sick. Instead, they are "cognitively wrong." That is, their thinking is flawed.[59]

The founder of reality therapy, William Glasser, believes that people are in a continual process of making choices. It is making poor choices that brings them misery, and there are better choices available to them. By using better thinking, people can prevent much of their own distress.[60] Albert Ellis, the originator of rational-emotive therapy, holds similar views. It is his contention that irrationality, or poor thinking, is responsible for many of our problems.[61]

The attitude that goes into problem-solving is just as important as the solution. A positive mental attitude toward problems is needed. We should view problems as opportunities for personal growth, learning, and the exercise of our ingenuity. There is nothing to be gained by considering them as misfortunes, the wrath of God, and so on. The negative perspective increases pain, dulls the imagination, saps vital energy into destructive depression, and weakens motivation.

We are not suggesting a naive approach to problems. Being optimistic about our success is not the same as being self-deluding. Just take a moment and reflect on some of the past problems in your life – particularly the ones that cost you sleepless nights and much agony. Where are they now? You prevailed, didn't you? But at the time you thought it was the end of the world.

BECOMING A PROBLEM-SOLVER

Since life is an endless series of problems, we need to be good problem-solvers. There are certain attitudes and practices that help in this regard.

- *Having confidence.* The attitude that you are always able to solve any problem that may come your way is indispensable. If not a full solution, a partial solution will do. Lacking confidence, on the other hand, guarantees defeat and defeat further erodes self-confidence.
- *Experiencing success.* Nothing succeeds like success, so the saying goes. And there is a lot of truth in that. How do you experience success when only failure comes your way, you say. Well, you can create your own successes. You start by tackling small problems. Once you taste success, your confidence increases and you'll be more motivated to succeed again. Success is the surest way of developing self-confidence and self-esteem. Self-confidence and self-esteem, in turn, are crucial to further success.
- *Seeing opportunities.* Another term for 'problem' is 'opportunity.' A life without problems is stagnant, unexciting, and simply not possible. Problems and challenges, on the other hand, present opportunities for accomplishments. There are few problems or challenges in life that are total disasters. Facing them as opportunities to grow, to achieve, to overcome will make a world of difference.
- *Learning.* We must learn skills that help meet our personal needs and enable us to relate to others.

PROBLEMS IN MARRIAGE

No marriage is problem-free. When the problem is between the couple and serious, certain conditions may arise and create a crisis situation. Here are some of the things that may happen.

● *Posturing.* Both sides take up their positions and antagonism appears. Each may posture, threaten, dare, and goad the other to do something. In this early phase, the posturing does not have much substance to it and may seem safe – since the antagonistic behavior may not yet be fully meant by either side. For instance, you may say, "That's the way it's going to be, take it or leave it. If you don't like it, talk to your lawyer and let us split." This may, at first, seem like an empty threat. But it may become a germ of a bad idea – to go ahead and talk to the lawyer about splitting.

● *Polarized thinking.* Thinking becomes polarized. Things are seen in black and white terms. Exaggerated bad qualities are ascribed to the other side – while failings on one's own side, even if highly relevant to the crisis, are overlooked. Each may see the other as bent on domination, as being unfair, insensitive, selfish, and incapable of making rational decisions. This mirror image effect distorts whatever the other does or says. This type of hostile preliminary is a prelude to destructive actions. By mentally preparing, the antagonists ready themselves for cruel and heartless actions to come.

● *Domination of emotions.* In crises, emotion not reason leads the charge. The rational mind, already clouded by intense emotions, deserts the individual when it is needed most. Emotional, poorly-thought-out words and actions aggravate an already explosive situation.

● *False justification.* As the rhetoric and posturing continues, the couple may start believing their own vituperation as the naked truth. This is a logical step in the illogical process of crisis behavior. There is a need to justify one's behavior and to keep the battle raging; it cannot be sustained without being self-convincing and self-deluding. Fact becomes almost irrelevant at this advanced stage of crisis. Posturing and rhetoric, if allowed to continue, will inevitably progress to the next stage – action – usually destructive and violent.

The best way to deal with crises is to prevent them in the first place. The next best thing is to do all you can to cool things down and reduce polarization.

FEATURES OF CRISIS SITUATIONS

A crisis is a problem that has gotten out of hand – a monster out of control ready and able to do a lot of damage. The following features characterize crisis situations.

- *Stress.* As the crisis emerges, stress begins to develop. Sometimes – particularly in the early stages – this may even be pleasurable, since it gives people a sense of importance, of being in action. It may bring some excitement in an otherwise dull marriage. Each may act decisively, feel a lot of energy, and do rash things.
- *Rigidity.* As crisis deepens, thinking becomes rigid, oversimplified, and dominated by emotion. The pair develops tunnel vision, becoming unable to see the other side's point of view. They opt for quick and easy fixes rather than looking at the long-term goals and consequences.
- *Mental constriction.* The range of alternative solutions shrinks. Thinking and planning becomes both superficial and short-term; each fails to anticipate what the other may do.
- *Disruption of concentration.* As the crisis continues, stress builds up and the ability to concentrate on the relevant features of the problem fades. The uncertainty of the situation leads to further anxiety, which makes the couple less effective in working out a rational solution.
- *Suspicion.* A sense of distrust and hurt, combined with antagonistic feelings, reduce the prospect of working out a fair compromise.
- *Crisis autonomy.* Once started and not immediately defused, the crisis takes on a life of its own – because each spouse is willing to believe in it, and fans the fire.
- *Neglect.* Individuals respond to crises by working harder in those areas that are directly relevant, in their view, to that crisis and they ignore other important aspects of their lives.

Unfortunately, many of the crises in marriage are caused needlessly – through negligence or immaturity – by the couples themselves. Although problems cannot be completely avoided, most crises can be. A good marriage will solve problems as they come along, without allowing them to gather crisis force; it does not create crises, and is likely to emerge undefeated from external ones – and even stronger than before.

▶ 19 ◀

CHAPTER

PERSONALITY & CONFLICT

Each of us is a unique mix of what we inherit from our parents and what we learn from our environment, that is, of genes and experience.[62] The genes are the raw material and experience is the force that selectively puts the bits and pieces together to make the person.

No two humans, even identical twins, are exactly alike, because no two humans ever experience exactly the same things in life. So compatibility is not about being perfectly alike – an impossibility. Compatibility is about being in agreement and harmony. Since personalities are different, conflicts are natural, and not all conflicts are bad or destructive. Conflicts arise when there are two different perspectives. In marriage, they can be reconciled by generating a third perspective that may even be more desirable than either of the original two.

Each human being's personality starts taking shape at birth. Various life demands require action. Some events just happen without us being their intended target, while others are specifically aimed for us, such as parental training. Soon, we realize the good, bad and indifferent consequences of the things we say and do. These consequences, in turn, play a powerful role in determining what we might say or do under similar circumstances in the future.

By marriage time, people are adults. Many years of interplay have gone on between the personality and environmental forces, so that a fairly stable personality core is in place. One person may be easygoing, another highly strung, another friendly, and so forth. Marriage is a crucial experience for both partners and how you deal with your spouse has a profound effect on his or her behavior and personality. So be alert to opportunities to reward desirable behavior and temperaments. By so doing you are likely to enhance them. Similarly, try not to reward undesirable behavior and temperaments.

SHADES OF PERSONALITY

Personality is not carved in granite. It is more like a relatively stable configuration of temperaments and dispositions. Each person has many shades of the same general personality. The contrast between shades may seem great – but it is still within the same range. When the shades become drastically different, then we have a case of split or multiple personality.

Everything and everyone has the potential of bringing out a particular shade of another person's character. The adage "He brings out the worst in me" refers to this capability. In fact, you may be a hundred somewhat different shades of yourself when you are with a hundred different people. This is perfectly normal. You are not being deceptive or two-faced, you are just reacting appropriately to a particular trigger – be it another person, a dog, or an event.

Fundamental to any successful relationship is evoking and nurturing the right shades in each other. Even saints are likely to have some shades of meanness, perhaps buried deeply. Given the right provocation, that bad version raises its head. So make a habit of doing what you can to bring out his or her better shades. The more this happens, the less effort it will take. The bad shades get buried deeper and are less likely to make their appearance. A couple of examples should clarify what we mean.

- You notice that your wife usually deals intelligently with rudeness, rather than reacting in kind. You can strengthen that quality by giving her a bear hug and saying, "Honey, I am impressed. I just love the way you handled that. It is so easy and tempting to react rudely to rudeness – that doesn't take any talent. But handling it the way you did is an art: putting an end to the rudeness without offending the person. Would you coach me? I really need to follow your example on this."

● You have a disagreement. She has been hinting about buying a new car and you don't think that she needs one. You feel that the money can be saved for something else. The hinting phase is over and decision time is at hand. Instead of relying solely on facts, you can call upon some of the shades of her personality that would become your ally in convincing her not to buy the car. You may want to proceed like this: "Honey, I really love the way you take your time – particularly when important decisions are involved – and think things through. You have such self-control. As far as this car is concerned, of course I want you to have everything that pleases you. I would also enjoy driving it from time to time. So let's use your sensible approach and see where we stand financially. I am sure that we'll make the wisest decision together."

That may help get her off the 'impulse-track' – not a positive personality shade – and on the 'thoughtful track' – something that we all need to be on.

PERSONALITY TYPES AND COMPATIBILITY

Life is about growth and marriage is a classroom where the couple are both the teachers and the pupils. Sometimes when two people are radically different, the difference may work for the marriage. For example, a hot-tempered person would get along best with a calm individual, so goes the reasoning. Or a dominant person will do best with a submissive type. But this kind of extrapolation from physics and the laws of magnetism is a chancy leap. In many instances it can work the other way, and two people of vastly different psychological make up may be very incompatible. The two may find themselves on opposite ends of every issue and the marriage becomes a constant battle.

TIPS ON CONFLICT RESOLUTION

Problems in marriage are of two types – those that pit the partners against each other and those that they must face together. Problems from one area can spill over into the other.

Conflict is at the heart of most problems, and as long as two or more people deal with one another, there will be conflict. Conflict arises from disagreements, and disagreements are rooted in differences of perceptions, opinions, and preferences. Conflicts are neither bad nor good. The way we go about resolving them and their eventual outcomes are the deciding factors. The best decisions and outcomes frequently result from the candid clash of differing views.

When your marriage is experiencing difficulties because you and your partner are stuck on opposite poles of an issue, try the following:

- *Role playing.* Sometimes it is helpful to use role playing – where you switch roles, you doing your best to convince him of the merits of his view and him trying to convince you of the virtues of your opinion. This strategy helps familiarize both of you with the pros and cons of each and will likely create a less polarized atmosphere for the eventual peaceful resolution of the disagreement.
- *People.* Try not to confuse problems with the people involved. The aim is to eliminate the problem, so make it a habit, early in marriage, to work as a team to solve a problem rather than trying to defeat each other. For example, there may be a problem about who is going to do the cooking. It is unwise for the wife to sound off, saying, "You men are all alike – exploitive, chauvinist, and old-fashioned. I thought that I was marrying an emancipated, enlightened human being. Here you are, no more liberated than your dad. You expect me to do all the cooking and no way am I going to do that." This mixing of people with problems creates polarization, digs deep psychological trenches, and is a potent call to war.[63] Even if the pair succeed in solving the problem, feelings of hurt will linger below the surface and will make the next battle even more destructive.

Instead, the couple should realize that neither of them is really the problem – the problem is cooking. They can work together and eliminate the problem. Perhaps by eating out more often, dividing the chore, making more use of convenience food, and so forth. Always attack the problem together and avoid attacking each other.

● *Issue*. Focus on the issue and strip it of all disguises. Sometimes people go to great lengths to come up with the silliest accusations and excuses to vent their frustration. Try to work your way through these smoke-screens and pinpoint the real issue. Then attack the problem together. For example, the husband may say that he wants to sleep in a separate bed because he can't sleep well with someone who tosses and turns all night. The wife vehemently objects, "I didn't get married to sleep by myself. How come, all of a sudden, I turn and toss all night? You are just a complaining wimp."

The issue, in fact, may be that the husband is worried about his sexual performance. A safe excuse is then produced to protect himself from both the physical demand and the psychological embarrassment.

But we should add a note of caution here. Don't get into the habit of automatically seeing a hidden motive in every word and action. Don't adopt the destructive practice of psychoanalyzing your spouse – reading all kinds of symbolism into everything. Sigmund Freud, who gave us all this, had a rich imagination and few facts in concocting his theory. So you shouldn't rely too heavily on theories that most experts now question.

● *Alternatives*. The worst thing to do in any disagreement is to stick with only one solution. Always work out several, more or less equally attractive options. The only options that should ever be considered in marriage are those that result in mutual gain. The win–win strategy should be the standard for all negotiations and decision-making in marriage.

● *Token behavior*. At times of tension, argument, and high emotions, it is important to do or say something that will tone things down – anything in the right direction is welcome. For example, a smile, a word of endearment, recollection of a funny episode, a hug, a non-accusatory reminder that past episodes of arguments have been such a waste of time. These token positive acts will serve to put out the fire and get the dialogue on a loving, united track.

● *Rhetoric*. In marriage, the rhetoric of belligerence is the most deadly thing next to physical violence. Words that are senseless, baseless, accusatory, threatening, divisive, disgusting, degrading, and emotionally charged make loving resolution very difficult, if not impossible. They always leave psychological wounds of various degrees – wounds that may bleed on subsequent occasions, and scars that may never heal.

An ancient anecdote drives this point home. Once upon a time there was a man who made his living by chopping, hauling, and selling wood. In the course of his daily work, he struck up a friendship with a lion that lived in the same forest. Every day, at noon, the woodcutter would settle in a shady spot and eat his bread. It was during this respite that the lion would appear, lie down next to him, and the two would have a conversation like the best of friends.

One day, as usual, the lion appeared and stretched out on the ground next to his woodcutter friend and they talked. Suddenly the woodcutter said to the lion, "Wow, my friend, today you have such stinking breath – it is so bad that I can hardly eat my bread." The unkind words infuriated the lion. He pounced on the woodcutter and mauled him badly. The woodcutter, bleeding profusely, managed to reach the village. It took a long time before he was able to go back again to the wood for his daily toil. The first day back in the wood, he sat in the familiar spot to eat his bread. As usual, the lion appeared and stretched out near him. The woodcutter welcomed his friend and assured him that the wounds had completely healed and that there was nothing to worry about. The lion observed, "But the wounds you inflicted on me with your sharp tongue are still bleeding inside me."

The moral of the story is the exact opposite of the nursery rhyme, "Sticks and stones can break my bones, but words can never hurt me." Words can hurt – they can hurt very badly and for a long time.

TACKLING PROBLEMS

Problems, conflicts, and disputes are constants of life – only the methods of dealing with them change. People try things; practices that work are kept and improved, and those that don't work usually drop out. This seemingly simple process is at the core of human progress and civilization. When it comes to problem-solving, there are at least four general methods.

- *Primitive*. Here, problems are settled by crude measures such as violence. A child, for instance, wanting another's toy, may just grab for it. If the owner resists, there may be pushing, shoving, and hitting. Adults also operate at this level when they engage in physical or verbal assault to intimidate or defeat an opponent. Other variations in this category include pouting, crying, threatening, throwing tantrums, not speaking to the person, or severing the relationship. This type of crude strategy is also employed at the level of groups and nations, when there are fights, wars, economic and other sanctions among nations.
- *Deceptive*. Attempts are sometimes made to solve problems and reach objectives by using deception in various forms. A child, for instance, may try to get another child's toy by distracting him. Or he may promise to share his candy while having no intention of doing so. Adults are masters of deception, and although it is potentially more treacherous, is a higher method of problem-solving than violence.
- *Manipulative*. This is a more sophisticated way of getting what we want, and involves manipulating people and situations. A child, for instance, may try to give his broken toy in a 'fair' exchange for another's brand new toy. Many forms of bargaining, negotiation, and contracts are examples of this strategy. It is guided by the principle of doing whatever is within the limits of the law to conclude the deal to your advantage. The other's interest is an irrelevancy or at best is secondary.
- *Consultative*. Consultation is a totally different practice. It is based on a revolutionary system of values and attitudes. It is not a 'me against you,' but a 'we against it' strategy. It is not a battle of wills, it is the meeting of a common challenge together for mutual benefit.

Consultation is working together to solve any problem in a way that would benefit both parties. Everyone wins when consultation is used, but consultation is harder to learn and practice because it is the most advanced method of conflict resolution and problem-solving. It is superior both because it is fair and because it produces the best results in the long run. See the following chapter for a discussion of consultation techniques.

This evolutionary process can be seen in the history of the species as well as in the course of a person's life – from pre-historical reliance on brute force to modern-day consciousness and concern about what is 'right' rather than what is right for 'me.'

Consultation is the most valuable tool for building a successful marriage. It is a tool for finding out the truth, solving problems, deciding on the best course of action, preventing difficulties, and generating new ideas and plans. It is a means of equitably sharing power and decision-making between two or more people. It is the tool of the new paradigm:

OLD PARADIGM	NEW PARADIGM
One-man decisions	Group decisions
Dictatorial behavior	Egalitarian behavior
Stratified rank	One rank
Competition	Cooperation
Autocracy	Shared governance
Adversarial behavior	Congenial behavior
Limited insight	Expanded insight
Poor group adherence	Good group support
Selfishness	Altruism
Pyramidal decision-making	Circular decision-making – input from all

RULES FOR MARITAL CONFLICT

Conflicts arise even in the most perfect of relationships. To deal with conflict in your marriage, we recommend two simple rules:

Rule # 1: Always resolve your differences amicably, lovingly and peacefully.

Rule # 2: In those instances where you fail to resolve your differences amicably, refer to Rule # 1.

▶ 20 ◀

CHAPTER

PRACTICING CONSULTATION

Whether the problem is between the two of you, such as a disagreement on doing the household chores, or coming from the outside, such as having to relocate to another town, you need to use consultation. Consultation is the most powerful tool for problem-solving, conflict resolution, and creation of a thriving marriage. It is the practice of two or more people pooling their intelligence, goodwill, and resources in a combined effort at assessing a situation, discovering the facts, generating options, making a decision, and together carrying out that decision to a successful conclusion.

Consultation is the key to a lifelong successful marriage. It is a process that confers equal status on the husband and wife in all aspects of their shared life. It empowers the pair far beyond what each is capable of accomplishing alone. Consultation allows free, candid, selfless exchanges of views, needs, and preferences between the couple. This pooling of the pair's resources creates *positive synergy* – making the outcome much superior to any decisions that could have been made individually.

Consultation constantly repairs the 'cracks' that develop, from time to time, in the relationship, and further strengthens the bond. Also, it has a number of other advantages that go beyond specific problem-solving and decision-making. Consultation trains everyone in thinking logically; becoming more articulate; listening more effectively to others and noticing feelings and emotions; discovering creative solutions; including ethical considerations in decision-making; learning to be candid, yet courteous; respecting others, their preferences, and views; and practicing the principles of the new paradigm – equality, cooperation and unity.

CONSULTATION AND EQUALITY IN MARRIAGE

The modern marriage has two equal partners, the wife and the husband. Shared responsibility and shared privilege are both indispensable and a cherished feature of a lifelong marriage. In the modern home, both husband and wife contribute, unlike the traditional patriarchal family where the husband made the important decisions. This may have made life simple, but simplicity is not always the answer. The new paradigm demands the more difficult, yet much superior, procedure of consultative decision-making. In most modern marriages the couple are equally well educated; both may be professionally employed outside the home, and equally skilled in solving complex problems. Hence, shared governance is in the best interests of the marriage, not only for the equality it creates between husband and wife.

It is a good idea for the couple to get into the habit of practicing consultation early on in their relationship, so that they can use and refine the skill over the years. When children arrive, they too should be included in the family consultation as soon as possible. Parents can consult even the very young on topics that they can understand and are of interest to them. As the children grow older and their capabilities increase, they should be included in more and more family decision-making. When children have a say in family decisions, they are much more likely to abide by them, and the entire family is more united and more in tune with the spirit of the age. Children who learn to use the powerful tool of consultation put it to good effect outside the home, and eventually as adults are aware of its benefits in the workplace and in their own marriage.

CONSULTATION ATTITUDES AND SKILLS

A number of skills and attitudes are necessary for effective consultation. Nine of them are listed below:

- *Mutual respect and fellowship*. We keep emphasizing the importance of respect in a successful marriage. Without respect for one another, there is little of value in the relationship. Consultation thrives on respect – genuine respect for the opinions, feelings, preferences, and contributions of the other.
- *Unselfishness and honesty*. Selfishness is most destructive to consultation. Consultation is not a tool or a forum for getting one's own way, it is an instrument for finding the best way – which is not always one's chosen or cherished plan. Do all you can to resist any tendency toward abusing the consultation process by playing games, conniving, and scheming – all in an effort to get your way. In the long run, it will backfire.
- *Willingness to speak*. In consultation, speaking is an obligation. Thoughts, feelings, preferences should all be expressed freely but with courtesy. Don't assume that your spouse gets the whole picture from a vague hint – then become disappointed when your wishes are not respected.
- *Listening*. It is easier to convince people to speak than to listen. But listening with your all to the concerns of your partner – as expressed in words, body language, and facial expressions – is vital to consultation.
- *Patience*. One of the most difficult qualities to acquire and practice, patience is a key to successful consultation. It is always easier to go ahead and do whatever you want than discuss things with others. Consultation has a price tag, and patience is part of the bill.
- *Speaking effectively*. The recommendation for speaking should not be taken as a license for rambling, confused and haphazard verbiage, and for taxing each other's patience. Certainly, there are times in marriage when you might want to do these things as part of letting your hair down. But in con-

sultation you need to organize your thoughts, be focused, and be as precise as you can in articulating your concerns. People usually consult about complicated problems, and the complexity of these problems is trying enough in itself. So make an effort to be lucid.

● *Harnessing egotism*. In a world that not only condones but promotes selfishness – by admonitions such as "Look after number one" – it is easy to become an egotist. We all have a strong disposition toward egotism anyway. Consultation demands that the couple park their egos outside before settling down to a good heart-to-heart and mind-to-mind exchange. So far as possible, consultation should be free of statements that create polarization and bruise the ego. Be careful – egos tend to bruise easily!

● *Creativity*. Be creative when generating ideas. At this stage anything goes. Let your imagination wing away to the farthest reaches of possibility. Concerns such as practicality, costs, and so on should come later. No idea should be ridiculed, for two reasons: it blocks the free flow, and it creates hurt feelings.

● *Non-offensiveness*. Try not to offend and guard against being offended easily. Develop a very thick skin for yourself, and always see the other person as having the thinnest skin.

ESSENTIAL STEPS OF CONSULTATION

There are seven steps to consultation.

1. *The subject*. The subject of consultation should be clearly specified right at the start. For example, how the couple can best handle household chores – or how to manage finances. Consultation can involve brainstorming, but the brainstorming should focus on a specified problem, issue, or concern.

2. *The facts*. Wise decisions and good solutions are seldom revelations. They are usually the result of hard work and knowing the facts. Questions and answers regarding who, what, where, why, when and how are central to the success of the deliberation.

3. *Relevance*. What are the ethical or moral, social, personal, and practical considerations concerning the issue?

4. *Options*. What are possible solutions, strategies, and plans? Generate as many options as possible – not just the solution that you have your heart set on or the one that is only to your advantage.

5. *Decision*. Evaluate each option with regard to costs in time, money, energy, and emotion. Choose the one most attractive to both of you.

6. *Action*. Get fully behind the selected decision and carry it out together. Success is most likely when the two of you work to accomplish your objective.

7. *Flexibility*. Once you make a decision, you are committed to it. Yet you need to be flexible; monitor progress, and make adjustments along the way when necessary to achieve your goal.

CONSULTATION SUMMARY

Most consultations in marriage are informal. This summary is a ready reference to remind us of the ingredients of consultation.

Attitudes and Skills:

- *Mutual respect*. Consult at all times with mutual respect.
- *Unselfishness & honesty*. Be unselfish. No scheming.
- *Willingness to speak*. Speaking is not only a privilege, it is an obligation.
- *Listening*. Listen sincerely and attentively.
- *Patience*. Don't rush things. Allow full airing of facts and views.
- *Speaking effectively*. Don't ramble. Organize and focus your thoughts.
- *Harnessing egotism*. Lock your egos out, and let ideas survive on merit.
- *Creativity*. Come up with wild ideas. Be as creative as you can.
- *Non-offensiveness*. Be considerate as well as open.

Steps to Consultation:

- *The subject*. Define the issue to be consulted upon.
- *The facts*. Who, what, where, when, why, and how?

- *Relevance*. What are the ethical, moral and social considerations relevant to the issue?
- *Alternatives*. What are the alternative solutions – the costs and benefits of each?
- *Decision*. Choose the best and work for it together.
- *Re-evaluate the decision after a fair trial period*. Make needed adjustments to achieve the goal.

▶ 21 ◀

CHAPTER

FINANCES

The belief that you can live on love is fuzzy thinking that lasts only until it is time for the next meal. Equally fuzzy is the belief in a material nirvana – the belief that money is the answer to everything. But the truth is that living in a material world requires material means, and financial difficulties and disagreements are a major cause of divorce.[20] Finances become even more critical in marriages where the couple must constantly scrape to make ends meet.[64] So the subject of money and finances deserves careful attention.

We advise the following:

- *Develop a budget*. This budget should list your anticipated income and expenses – both short- and long-term. Live within your budget, and don't spend ahead of your earnings. Don't talk yourself into foolish expenditure.
- *Save regularly*. No matter what your income is, you should save a certain percentage of it for potential loss of income, the education of children, old age, emergencies, and as protection against inflation. How much should you save? We recommend a minimum of ten percent of your gross income. Just go ahead and make do without this amount – as

if you didn't have it in the first place. Savings not only provide financial security, they give you peace of mind as well. When you have some savings, you are less likely to be in a constant state of apprehension over finances.

You can also earmark what you want to use your savings for. You should consult together on your short-term and long-term financial needs and objectives, things such as a new washing machine, a vacation, children's education, or a reserve for retirement.

• *His and hers arrangement*. If at all possible, have a common family fund, not a his and hers mentality. No separate checking accounts unless it is necessary for business requirements or tax records. No individually owned cars, stocks and bonds, real estate, and so on. The complete sharing of finances is an inseparable part of the total sharing that a successful marriage is all about.

• *Frugality*. In materially affluent societies, the past decades have seen a surge in consumption – depleting many of the planet's irreplaceable resources. Avid consumerism is also aggravating the problems of polluting the land, the air, and the waterways. Psychologically, consumerism can produce the chronic suffering that is marked by insatiable appetite and never-ending dissatisfaction. The materially very rich are often afflicted with the disease of affluence – affluenza.

We recommend frugality as a practice that is less taxing on the resources of the planet, on the average family's budget, and on your psychological well-being. There is an immense satisfaction in owning only a few pairs of shoes, for example, even when you are able to afford many. It is a soul-soothing act to avoid wasting food – to make do with as little of everything as possible.

• *Buying on credit*. The world is becoming increasingly dependent on plastic money. Credit cards and electronic transfers are rapidly replacing cash currencies. Also, it is becoming increasingly easy to borrow small and large amounts. We advise against credit purchases and borrowing with only a few exceptions.

If you wish to use a credit card for its convenience and relative safety, you should limit its use to items provided for in your budget – and pay it off, without accruing interest charges. Borrowing should be done with extreme care and limited to essentials such as the down-payment for a home, meeting an emergency health expense, or paying educational expenses. No money should be borrowed to pay for vacations and luxury items. All such expenditures must come from budgeted savings.

Putting finances on a solid footing is a task that no marriage can afford to neglect.

INEQUALITY OF EARNINGS

In a materialistic world, money is the yardstick of worth. By this yardstick, women are undervalued. In the United States, for instance, women earn roughly 75 cents for every dollar earned by men. Women's lower earning power in the workplace implies that their work and time – hence, they themselves – are less valuable. This inequality of earning is due to the fact that women usually work in less prestigious jobs. Even when doing the same or comparable work, women are still paid less than men.[9]

This is a case of the old paradigm still at work – a double standard that kept women in subservience. Women's second-class status in the workplace pegs them in a subordinate role at home also. The man, by virtue of his greater earnings, is considered the head of the household. In the new paradigm, there are two equal co-heads – the wife and the husband, irrespective of earnings or any other consideration. Being a woman or a man matters in marriage only when it comes to making babies. The rest of the time they are simply humans.

FINANCIAL MANAGEMENT

There are many useful books on the subject of managing money and family finances. It is a good idea to read them. We particularly like an excellent book by Harold Moe.[65] It is written in simple language with the aim of showing individuals and families how to budget their finances. Many couples need to go beyond the fundamental practice of budgeting, and for them additional reading and consulting with investment counselors are essential tasks. Pressures of time, laziness, or lack of interest can spell disaster for couples who go carelessly about their savings and investments. Some may simply play it safe, and just pour everything into a savings account. This is not necessarily the best practice if you are paying taxes on the interest and the interest hardly covers the rate of inflation. Others may be victimized by greed – the allure of making a big fortune – and invest their savings in risky or fraudulent ventures.

We recommend prudence in managing money. It is better to err on the side of safety than to lose one's savings in an ill-conceived venture. There are times when you need to go beyond your neighborhood banker for sensible investment of your savings, and in these instances, you should always deal with well-established institutions of sound reputation, institutions that have been around for a while, are endorsed by the chamber of commerce and certified by national financial guilds and associations.

MATERIALISM AND MARRIAGE

We all have our fantasies – some are comforting, as if the mind were 'drugging' itself to experience a high. Others are a means of escaping from unpleasant reality and may be harmless. But others can be destructive.

Many fantasies remain in our subconscious, at the back of our thoughts. We are not directly aware of them. Yet, they influence our thoughts, our actions, and our feelings. Men and women enter marriage with loads of fantasies. Many of these 'expectations' are common to both genders, while some are exclusive to each sex. Gender differences in these expectations are the result of acculturation that indoctrinates men and women along different lines. With respect to marriage, men fantasize unrealistically about a wife who is a perfect home-maker, a magnificent lover, a first-class mother, an unsurpassed cook, a tireless cleaning lady, and a domestic manager who is on duty around the clock.

Women have their own set of fantasies or unrealistic expectations. They expect the man to be a perfect husband and an excellent provider – somehow managing to make a lot of money to serve the needs and wants of his family.

Unfortunately, there is always a gap between the world of fantasy and the world of reality. The greater the gap, the greater the resulting frustration and unhappiness. We live in a materialist culture – a culture dominated by an insatiable desire for consumption and experience. Most husbands fail to provide for their family at the fantasized level, and when this happens, the wife consciously or unconsciously feels disappointment, and is likely to lose her respect for the 'unworthy' spouse. Where there is no respect, love and the loving relationship can hardly thrive.

What happens to a relationship where materialistic concerns are overemphasized depends on a number of factors. We would like to say a few words about two of the possibilities.

- *Delaying marriage*. Some couples delay their marriage for years to amass the money that they feel is necessary for getting married. Obviously we are not objecting to the prudent pairs who plan their finances together so that they have the required funds. We are referring to those who have ample funds, yet don't think they do and strive for more.
- *The wife plunging in*. When the couple are married and material expectations are not met, the wife may sacrifice the all-important task of raising and educating the children – not for professional satisfaction, but for bringing home more money. In this instance, the consequences are particularly disastrous. Although the wife's added income services the family's appetite, the husband – often unconsciously – feels humiliated by failing to be the sole breadwinner of the family. Meanwhile the wife feels a measure of economic independence, but at a steep cost that includes trusting the children to others for long hours and experiencing the anxiety of separation. She also may feel alienated from her 'failed man.'

When both partners work outside the home full-time, even when they have no children, they sacrifice a great deal at the altar of materialism. Frequently, the couple spends the evening trying to recover from the hassles of their daily chase, preoccupied with their respective job-related problems, and hardly in a condition to nurture their companionship and love.

When children are involved, the early years of entrusting them to babysitters and nursery schools are followed by years of time alone at home or in the company of other children in a similar situation. The children can hardly be expected to develop into spiritually, emotionally, and intellectually healthy human beings without the presence of loving parents. The parents feel guilty for having neither the time nor the energy their children require. To assuage their guilt, they do the only thing they can and know how to do: they throw money at the children, who use it to 'buy' the substitutes for parental love and time – alcohol, drugs, fashionable clothes, and so on.

WHAT TO DO?

We personally believe in the complete equality of men and women in marriage or in any other area of life. We don't believe that the man should always be the breadwinner and the woman the home-maker. We described above the age-old fantasies and expectations that permeate the unconscious of the two genders and direct our behavior. Once we realize their effect, then we can deal with the problem. Here are some possibilities.

- *Harnessing materialism*. Work hard to scale down on the elusive and insatiable desire for material things and experiences. As Mahatma Gandhi said, "there is enough to meet everyone's need, but not enough for everyone's greed."
- *Abandoning stereotypes*. Men and women are equal partners who bring their respective gifts to a common venture. Each couple should chart its own life course according to its own resources and aspirations – free from the fetters of traditional role assignment.
- *Joint planning*. There is nothing wrong with both partners working to amass the needed funds to start a family –

as long as amassing funds does not become an end in itself. There is nothing wrong with the husband assuming the major role for child-care while the wife works on a job, if that arrangement serves the family's best interest. Hence, it is wise to take a little time and consult together about your priorities, your work opportunities, and the lifestyle that you want. Make sure that neither money, essential as it is, nor traditional obsolete thinking dictate your decision.

PART SiX

PROTECTING MARRIAGE

Marriage is a great investment of our emotions – the culmination of years of dreaming and planning. There is no reason for this sweet hope to sour – or end in divorce – if the couple works together to protect it. In this section we talk about ways of protecting and nurturing the marriage bond, avoiding things that undermine it, and reaping the rewards of your joint labor. We provide some insight into the human mind, suggest ways of handling arguments, point out common deadly traps and show you alternatives to destructive tendencies. We discuss methods that can help you make your marriage a true haven of happiness – strong, vibrant, and able to sustain you in the inevitable hard times. We talk about other relationships, with relatives, friends and children, and about social obligations and how to handle them.

▶ 22 ◀

CHAPTER

THE MARRIAGE RELATIONSHIP

A successful marriage is about two people bonding with each other in a lifelong, satisfying relationship. To succeed in marriage, we need know-how, motivation, and a bit of luck. In this section, we share some tips on human nature – things that work for and work against two people becoming close and staying close.

We are what we believe we are. And what we believe has a lot to do with what we do and what we become. Many studies, including the work of psychologist Albert Bandura,[66] document the importance of beliefs in directing our lives. To have a good marriage, you have to believe that a good marriage is possible in the first place, that you want to have a good marriage and that you are willing to work for it.

FIVE RULES OF A GOOD RELATIONSHIP

In marriage, or in any relationship, there are some golden rules to keep in mind. Five of them are listed below:

Rule #1: Don't allow the other person determine what you do or say. Be an actor, not a reactor.
Rule #2: Don't rush into saying or doing something that you might later regret – think things through.

Rule #3: Don't paint yourself or the other person into a corner – always leave a way out.
Rule #4: Don't be short-sighted – keep an eye on the long-term consequences of your words and actions.
Rule #5: Don't be unfair – because you expect to be treated fairly.

UNDERSTANDING THE MIND

It is said that we live in the mind. It is true that the mind is at the center of everything. Understanding how the human mind works is crucial for understanding ourselves and dealing with others. Here are a few insights that are relevant to our discussion.

- *Making sense*. It is the mind – like a supercomputer – that makes sense out of billions of haphazard sensory inputs pouring into it. It does this by sorting things out, classifying them, and connecting them with its past experiences as well as its preferences.
- *Deception*. The mind is one big deception machine. All organisms make use of deception but humans do it better. A major function of the mind is to deceive, rearrange facts and achieve a certain objective. Deceptions of various degrees and kind are the basic products of the mind. Euphemism, tact, flattery, the advertising and packaging of goods and a host of other human activities involve various amounts of deception. In a real sense, being deceptive is being human – the natural way of behaving. It is being honest and forthright that must be learned and practiced – with great effort.
- *Self-deception*. The mind, so adept at deceiving others, fools itself on a regular basis. These deceptions run the whole gambit, from minor and inconsequential to major and problematic. The mind does not passively accept everything it sees – since not all facts meet its preferences and biases. In some cases, it relents and takes the facts for what they are. Equally often, it resorts to what amounts to self-deception. It does all kinds of manipulation and massaging to make the facts fit its fancy. An alcoholic who refuses to accept the fact that he has

a serious problem with alcohol is deceiving himself. So is the person who has a weight problem and is outgrowing his suit-pants – when he blames the change on the cleaner's carelessness.

● *Buying peace of mind.* Mental harmony and peace of mind are closely related. Mental harmony aims at reconciling the seemingly irreconcilable – like facts that don't fit our prejudices. Buying peace of mind, on the other hand, is a broader operation that involves producing psychological tranquilizers. The chief concerns here are anxiety and stress. We have discussed this subject elsewhere, and here just one example is enough. *Rationalization* is a universal way of producing psychological tranquilizers, and a classic mind trick that everyone uses. The aim is to get rid of unpleasant anxiety. People use rationalization particularly when they want to justify their foolish actions and in easing hurts or disappointments. And it is all done in the mind.

Consider the case of a newly married couple strapped for funds. The husband – without consulting his wife — buys a very expensive imported car on installment plan. This is not a very smart move, and he knows that he has put himself and his wife in a financial straitjacket – so the mental battle begins. He establishes superficial peace of mind by proclaiming to himself – and to his shocked wife – that his motive was to buy reliable transportation!

Or take the case of a woman who was hoping to get a well-deserved promotion. For whatever reason, she is by-passed and the promotion goes to someone across the hall. This is a blow to the woman's self-esteem. She is disappointed and anxious. What would her husband think? Would he value her less now? The mental agony created by these worries and disappointments can be soothed by the well-honed trick of rationalization. She convinces herself that she really didn't want the promotion. She reasons that the promotion would have been such a headache and would have put a lot of stress on her marriage – since she is also hoping to start a family soon. She would tell her husband that not getting the promotion was a blessing in disguise. This is the old sour grapes story, but it works, and works with amazing effectiveness.

MARRIAGE AND THE MIND

The mind is that elusive chief executive running our lives. It perceives the world, makes good or bad judgments, and determines how we feel and what we do. We can learn to control and direct the mind to work for us.

Among the things that the mind does in a day's work is a great deal of fantasizing – day-dreaming, distorting, and mental acrobatics. It does these things to make the fare of life more palatable. It is said that idle hands do the work of the devil – and the idle mind directs that work. The mind needs to be busy with something. If you don't give it something to do and focus its attention on, it will create its own work – not all of it good. So take charge and put your mind to do good work. Don't let it draw you into a world of fantasy. Don't allow it to dwell on all the bad things of life. Don't let it drag you into a dark mood.

We can be victimized by our own minds. In marriage, for instance, unrealistic expectations, baseless fantasies, unwarranted idolizing of the spouse are some of the dangers. Disappointment and disillusionment – poisons to relationships – are the results of unmet expectations. To make your marriage the best that can be takes a lot of doing, and it is all worth it. You need to protect your marriage not only from the assaults of the outside world but also from the natural trickeries of your own mind. Keep a level head. Love her or him for what she or he is, and keep mental trickery under control.

NOURISHING THE RELATIONSHIP

There are lots of do's and don'ts that go into building a solid and satisfying relationship. Some important do's are listed here.

- *Defining*. Define your spouse positively. That is, make an inventory of all the positive qualities that your partner has – include even those that are hardly there. Try to leave out the negative qualities from the definition. By defining your spouse positively, you act nicely toward him or her. This acting nicely, in turn, will prompt the other to reciprocate in kind and the relationship thrives.

● *Talking.* See to it that your busy life doesn't crowd out talk times. Make sure that both of you spend some time talking and sharing your thoughts and feelings. Criticisms, expressed or implied, are absolutely taboo during these important bonding talk sessions. This is the time for gently – with each other's help – putting down the burdens of the day as well as some of the ones you have been carrying around for a time.

● *Expressing.* Gently but clearly express how he or she can help, what is it that you want and are not getting. Don't count on your spouse to be a mind-reader. Help your spouse to give more to you by telling where he or she can be of most service to your needs. This relieves tension and builds trust.

● *Caring.* Show that you care. Show it in action, as well as words. When you reveal to each other your concerns, work hard to see if there isn't a way of helping with the problems. Come up with a suggestion, a help, a solution – if you can.

● *Accepting.* Fundamental to a good relationship is the assurance that you give the other that you accept and love him just the way he is. It is this assurance that is needed as a springboard for any desired change. Disapproval shuts the door on further intimacy.

● *Winning.* Winning is very important psychologically and biologically. Create situations for each other to win, rather than succumbing to the temptation of defeating your partner on every occasion that you possibly can. Defeat is as bitter as victory is sweet. Studies have shown that men who receive attention (winning affection) from women or who win in competitions show significantly higher testosterone levels. Women equally benefit from winning.

● *Favors.* "There is no duty more indispensable than that of returning kindness," says Cicero. Human beings are strongly inclined to reciprocate favors.[67] In many instances, a small favor can produce large returns, and the same principle operates between husband and wife. So, do each other favors.

Over the long run, you will both receive substantial returns on your investment.

● *Intimacy*. Intimacy – at the heart of a good marriage – is about freely sharing feelings and thoughts with someone you trust. Someone who will not betray you, ridicule you, moralize at you, or think less of you for revealing yourself. This is a very tall order. How can we disclose ourselves – reveal our deepest fears and even quirks to another – yet expect the other to respect us as much as before and not betray our trust? There is no way of achieving intimacy while keeping things secret. Disclosure always brings risks, but if we want intimacy, we must take some risks.

Fundamental to intimacy is the attitude that neither is perfect – that mutual, free sharing will help bring you closer and increase your love for each other.

INVESTING IN RELATIONSHIPS

We bring to any relationship two kinds of capital – words and actions. Think of the relationship as a tree. Good words and good deeds feed and water it; bad words and bad deeds poison and destroy it. We all know that action is important, but why words? Because they stand for feelings and possible actions.

You may ask, "Well, what if I really don't feel like saying nice things – isn't it better to be candid than forcing yourself to be nice? There are no pretenses with me. What you see is what you get." Being yourself and being insensitive, non-caring, and lazy are not the same thing. So irrespective of how you feel, make an effort to do and say nice things. At the very least, avoid saying and doing bad things.

A successful marriage is dynamic – it is responsive to change, evolving, and maturing. It is rooted in a stable core that allows adjustment as the couple pass through the phases of life from being newly weds, to being parents of young children, to the middle age, to the golden years. All along, the demands and opportunities facing the marriage change, and the couple accommodate and make the best of these inevitable shifts.

A healthy marriage relationship is a mix of intimacy and independence. Psychologist Carl Rogers writes about this seemingly paradoxical aspect of marriage, which is what makes for a truly rewarding relationship. "When each partner is making progress toward becoming increasingly his or her own self – the relationship becomes more enriching and satisfying."[2] This type of relationship is at the heart of the New Marriage Paradigm. It not only recognizes the legitimacy of individuation, it strives to facilitate it.

MENTAL TEMPLATES

Two people cannot travel together in the journey of life for very long unless they are both heading for the same destination, using the same road-map and sharing a great deal in common. Yet no two people ever see everything in exactly the same way, simply because each person has his or her own unique *mental template*. A mental template is the sum total of the person's feelings, knowledge, past experiences, preferences and beliefs. A template is a standard pattern against which things are compared. In the case of a mental template, the pattern is dynamic; by and large, the mental template responds to minor changes while retaining an overall stability.

Each time we encounter something, it is run instantaneously through the template and some kind of verdict emerges: "I like it," "I hate it," "I can take it or leave it," "It's not important," "I ought to do something about it," are only a few examples of the conclusions reached. Even being not sure or confused are outcomes. Inputs come from the outer as well as the inner world. When they come from the inner world, the template is examining some of its own contents, perhaps modifying itself, discarding some parts, and creating new components. An example is when we suddenly have an insight into something, without any new information coming from the outside world.

An indispensable provision of the journey of togetherness is having a common view of the world. When two people embark on a relationship, they begin with some things in common. If this initial common view is significant enough, then marriage may follow. The initial common view continues to expand in fulfilling lifelong marriages by the couple: talking together and comparing notes; by both of them intelligently modifying their respective mental templates to create greater harmony; by the realization that their falling in love, in the first place, is in part the result of some shared common views that can be further built upon.

Having a common view of the world – which is not the same thing as being perpetually in total agreement – is based on an understanding of each person's point of view. This understanding, a comprehension of how the other feels and from what experiences and backgrounds the other is drawing feelings and perceptions, is what is valuable. In other words, we may not agree on our perceptions, but we each understand where the other is 'coming from.'

Where there is enough of a common view of the world, the couple form a *mutual mental template*, and this is a priceless psychological anchor in a complex, erratic, and even crazy world. Now, they can run things through their mutual template whenever they are not sure of their own judgment or there is a need for confirmation. There is so much complexity, fragmentation, and even contradiction (cultural, social, economic and ethnic) in life that one desperately needs to have a lifelong partner who agrees on a whole set of 'givens' that ensure common responses to other people and situations. This shared template is good for one's mental health; it is reassuring not to feel all alone in one's perceptions. The shared template also provides for a check on reality. When baffled by life's frequent absurdities and unrealities, one can check with the partner that indeed one is not losing touch with reality.

All couples need the mutual template to function best in day-to-day life. Those who are not married aim to fill this need by forming close friendships, but in the case of couples, the mutual template is likely to be more comprehensive and more profound; it provides a 'home-base' of stability to return to psychologically.

If the couple fails to nurture their common view of the world by not regularly sharing perceptions and ideas and not being responsive to change, the marriage bond is jeopardized. The relationship weakens, the pair may remain poorly connected, and divorce becomes a real possibility.

IMPACT OF BAD EXPERIENCES

No matter what you enjoy in life – for example, eating, reading, making love – that enjoyment can be diminished, or even destroyed, if enough bad experiences become connected with it. For instance, you may love to eat fish. But if every time you eat it you get sick, you'll soon begin to dislike fish and avoid eating it. Or you may enjoy reading. Yet every time you sit down to read, he picks a fight with you. Soon, you fear reading and you lose your love for it. You enjoy making love, but, time and again your lovemaking involves significant emotional or physical pain. Gradually you lose your interest in sex. This reaction can become generalized to other activities and people, particularly if you experience the same pain with them. You don't even have to be consciously aware of what is really going on, and you might not be able to explain why, for example, you lost your love of reading. All you know is that you don't enjoy it any longer.

If two people are strongly attracted to each other they are likely to stay together. If attraction does not exist, the two are likely to go their own separate ways. A successful relationship is the one that starts out with an attraction that increases over the years. The original attraction is the capital with which a relationship starts, and what happens to it depends on how wisely the partners work with it. Some start with little and make a fortune, while others start with a fortune and squander it away. Of course it is always better to start with great attraction and compatibility.

At the practical level there are certain do's and don'ts that enhance attraction or destroy it. Think of any relationship as a joint bank account; all the nice things that you do and say to each other are deposits that build it up, while all the bad things that you do and say are like the withdrawals of your capital. When the withdrawals become more than the sum of the deposits, the account will collapse and the relationship may end. Therefore if you want your marriage to succeed you must say and do those things that make your partner feel good. Remember that we feel good about those who make us feel good. We also feel bad about those who make us feel bad.

Your feeling good depends on:

- you, yourself. What you do and what you don't do;
- others – how they interact with you;
- and you, again – how you take things and how you react to others.

So it starts and ends with you. Yet the middle part is also important – what others do or say to you, as well as the circumstances of your life. Also, actions and words provoke reactions in kind. If you want to keep your relationship happy and strong, use positive actions and words and get rid of the negatives.

▶ 23 ◀

CHAPTER

LEARNING & CHANGING

Long before getting married, people experience socialization. And at the heart of socialization is the handling of relationships – learning the intricacies involved in staying in the good graces of parents, getting along with siblings and forming friendships. Successful negotiation of these demands importantly determines one's quality of life. Further, it prepares the person for the most important relationship in life – the marriage relationship. Yet, there are more lessons to be learned, new practices to adopt and some old habits to discard in the building of a good lifelong marriage.

FRIENDSHIP VS. MARRIAGE

Two different sets of rules govern friendship and marriage. When two people become friends, there is a tacit understanding that they accept and enjoy each other basically just the way they are. Of course, the two friends may see flaws and shortcomings, but they generally conclude that they value the person as a package – even though parts of it may not be to their liking. Thus the friendship thrives – two people accepting and valuing each other with little or no attempt to improve each other.

In marriage, on the other hand, the relationship often takes the form of a crusade – one spouse likes certain things about the partner, finds other things marginal, and yet others intolerable. Human beings have a powerful tendency to try to change things to their liking. Trying to change your partner leads to a lot of battles, and one consequence of these battles is that you may in fact be making those faults and flaws even harder to overcome and making change less likely. Most behaviors are long-standing habits – they have deep and widespread roots, and cannot easily be uprooted. If you persist in your criticism, you are likely to create hard feelings. Criticism is a psychological ax – when used carelessly, it chops at the root of the relationship.

The marriage relationship must above all else be a relationship of true friends – honest acceptance of the person as a package of the good, the bad, and the average. Improving each other should be a secondary aim and done with extreme care, gentleness, and subtlety – making sure that the relationship doesn't degenerate into that of parent–child, teacher–pupil, angel–mortal. You must keep it at the level of total love, acceptance and parity. Then you can improve together as a team.

MODELING

"Monkey see, monkey do" is an old and true saying. Research shows that modeling our behavior on that of others can influence us in three different ways.[68]

- *Learning by watching*. We learn things by observing other people. Role models can also be found in pictures, films, books, or television. We may learn how to cook an exotic meal by watching it being done on television; we may learn to fear a vampire by seeing a horror movie; we develop attitudes about women or men by reading.
- *Weakening or strengthening*. Modeling may weaken or strengthen inhibitions. For instance, when a man notices other women's negative reactions to sexist comments, he is less likely to make sexist comments himself. Conversely, if

another man is rewarded for making sexist comments, the observer is more likely to do the same.

● *Prompting*. The actions of others may serve as prompts. For instance, seeing that another man is getting away with abusive behavior may encourage the observer to participate in it. Conversely, seeing that another's spouse severely rebukes his or her partner for abusiveness may have a suppressing influence on the observer's tendency to be abusive toward his or her own spouse.

Becoming what we are – to a large degree – is done through this process of modeling, in the home of our parents, and in early years. Modeling keeps on influencing us for the rest of our lives. Early in marriage, living in our own home, we need to create conditions and opportunities that provide desirable modeling. For instance, we should choose our friends wisely, avoid trash in movies and television, and act kindly ourselves.

ROLE-PLAYING

"All the world's a stage, /And all the men and women merely players./ They have their exits and their entrances;/And one man in his time plays many parts."[69]

Of course there are differences between the theatre of actors and the theatre of life. In real life, roles are broader, more numerous, and sometimes poorly defined. Yet each of us is a role-player in the drama of life. In life, a man or woman has a number of roles beside that of being a husband or wife. And the types of roles that they play importantly influence the quality of their lives. The taking on of roles is influenced by many factors – other people's expectations, the situation, and our own resources and inclinations.

● *Role-taking*. This is a process of self-evaluation – changing and devising our behavior to conform with the expectations of others. For instance, the husband, in a new marriage, is likely to adopt a domestic role that is in line with the wife's expectations. If she expects him to be an equal partner, a kind friend, and helpful around the house, that's the role he is likely to adopt.

- *Role-making*. Since each of us has to play numerous roles – some of them conflicting – we need to make adjustments in the various roles to make them consistent with our overall personality. For instance, a kind and compassionate person cannot have cruel and heartless roles, unless it's a case of multiple personality. So adjustments have to be made to create an overall consistency.
- *Role strain*. There are times when we have trouble meeting the requirements of a role. For instance, the woman who is expected to be a devoted wife, an exemplary mother, and a tireless volunteer for charities may fall apart under the strains of these multiple roles.
- *Role conflict*. This is a form of role strain involving incompatible roles. A woman who is expected to be a model home-maker and, at the same time, to be devoted to her professional career, experiences conflict between two largely incompatible roles.

THE BOSSING IMPULSE

People like to tell each other what to do. Parents tell children all about it, older siblings boss about the younger ones, teachers instruct pupils – so it goes. To carry on with this business of instruction in marriage is a natural extension of what is done everywhere else. And being bossy is a very easy habit to get into.

Some occupations by their very nature reinforce bossiness. For example, teachers, police officers, and factory supervisors tell others what to do and what not to do, as part of their jobs. Others such as the eldest child, the only child, or those who had lived alone for many years may have a greater disposition toward bossiness. Even so-called wimps can be very bossy, if given a chance. Being bossy feeds that part of our nature that wants to dominate, intimidate, and establish superiority. Frequently this bossiness is disguised as caring and wanting the best for others. There is, indeed, a very thin line between caring and being bossy. Of course you want to remind your spouse to take her medication if she tends to forget. That's caring. But you don't need to tell her to take the medication if she never forgets – this is an example of bossing disguised as caring.

Bossiness is a form of dominance. Dominance is seen in action in just about every species; the so-called 'pecking order' is not confined to chickens. For example, strict and elaborate hierarchies rule primates' social organizations. In monkeys, for instance, one strong male dominates the entire troupe. He works hard to maintain his position; he must take the lead in battles, be first to ward off predators, and constantly meet the challenge of other males intent on replacing him. But the rank has its rewards. He gets to eat what he wants and when he wants, and to mate with the female of his choice.

Bossiness, a human version of the dominance instinct, still bestows privileges, usually at a price. In the family, for instance, if you want to be the boss, then you must shoulder all the responsibilities that go with being the sole ruler of the household. Of course we recommend against it; the family with one head of the household is part of the old paradigm. Single parents are the first to tell us, from experience, that it is better by far to have an equal, caring and sharing partner than to be the sole ruler of the household.

HABITS

Habits are important because they save time and energy. Also, habits – good or bad – become habits because they work, and breaking a habit, something that has worked time and again, is not easy.

The habits of the couple are important to their marriage because they are the most likely way of doing things. Good habits, therefore, can be invaluable, while bad ones are trouble. For example, a man who routinely helps with chores is exercising a positive habit, while another man who leaves the table as soon as he is finished – without helping – is also acting habitually. Where do we acquire our habits? In the school of life. And marriage is certainly the home classroom of that school. A good marriage creates the conditions that foster a large set of good habits and gently dismantle the bad ones.

How can one instill good habits in another person without being bossy – which we have warned against – and dismantle the bad ones without taking an ax to the relationship? The best way to do it is by the proper use of reward. We said earlier that both good and bad habits are formed because they are efficient ways of doing things and they work. They are rewarding because they reduce the required effort or displeasure, or make the person feel good. Wise use of reward – both the withholding and the dispensing of it – can produce powerful results. We cannot give a recipe for the use of reward in every conceivable situation. You need to use your own good judgment in selecting the type of reward, the amount, and the timing for delivering or withholding it. Appropriate rewards are many and varied – praise, hugs, and treats are examples.

Your spouse, for instance, may be in the habit of writing checks without entering the amounts in the ledger, waiting for the bank's monthly statement to balance the account. You can see that this practice has somehow worked well enough for him to become a habit. It is not a good habit, nor can you tolerate it in your joint account. Sometimes, simply sharing your concern – in a non-critical way – is all that is needed for a change of the habit. At other times, you may be astounded how individuals resist changing even the simplest and seemingly trivial habits. In all such instances where resistance is encountered, there is need for sensitivity and patience. In the checkbook example, if a simple request fails, you may offer to do the entering and tactfully get your partner involved in the process. He may then surprise you and make an entry on his own. That calls for a hug, a kiss, or praise.

Not all habits are etched in granite, and they can be changed, some easily and others with great difficulty. Our advice is to avoid trying to change your partner and re-cast him or her as your ideal spouse. Chances are that you'll fail and so will the marriage. Work with those habits that are destructive or intolerable, but do it with wisdom, patience, and extreme care.

▶ 24 ◀

CHAPTER

THE MARRIAGE BOND

The bond that connects the husband and wife together can be thought of as a rope. When the partners are kind to each other, nurture one another, and make each other feel good, they keep adding more strands to the rope and the bond becomes stronger. Conversely, as they hurt or criticize each other, the strands begin to fray. If enough strands fray, the rope will eventually snap.

Constant strand-making, fraying, and patching goes on in marriage. For instance, when you say something nasty to your spouse, one strand may break. Then you may feel bad about what you have done and apologize. This apology and a hug may patch up the snapped strand, but it is not likely to be as strong as it was before. Another insult, even a minor one, may snap it again – making re-patching more difficult and the repaired strand much more susceptible to being snapped easily next time.

True love is the care you take in protecting every strand that ties you to your partner – the absence of any need for apology. When you don't snap any strands in the first place, there is no need for patching.

Yet humans are not perfect and we do and say things that can hurt each other's feelings. In these instances, it is much better to say you are sorry and apologize immediately – patching the frayed strand is better than showing false pride and letting the relationship take a beating. A patched strand is much better than no strand. An important thing about patching strands is that it should be done right away to minimize the damage, because hurt feelings have a way of recruiting energy and causing a great deal of damage. So, don't wait to hug him or her on Sunday! Do it now. This is preventive medicine, and needs to be administered long before the virus of hurt and disaffection begins to incubate and take hold. This is one instance where being patient is not a virtue – it is a vice. The successful relationship is the one that keeps on constantly adding new strands, while fraying or snapping as few as possible.

INVESTING EXCLUSIVELY IN THE SPOUSE

Under the old paradigm, the wife had little identity of her own – she became a part of the husband. She was not allowed to own property, not permitted to vote, and in some places barred from receiving an education. Some modern marriages create their own restrictions. For example, a couple may become excessively possessive of each other and avoid activities that don't include them both.

A successful marriage involves a bonding that is strong yet flexible. It not only allows full independence, but encourages each to soar as high as they can. There is so much worthwhile work in the larger world that must be done – so much to explore and learn, so much to share and shoulder. A strong marriage will create conditions that encourage the individuation of the partners – their becoming and doing their very best in a broad spectrum of life. Investing exclusively in one's spouse, no matter how wonderful it may be, is still a finite investment. It is also a risky investment. What if something happens to your spouse? You must still go on with life.

BETTER NICE THAN RIGHT

In relationships it is more important to be nice than to be right. Relationships are bonds of mutual support, more than anything else. So when you argue, when you try to prove him or her wrong, when you want to show off how much you know and how right you are, you are undermining the relationship.

Besides, much of the time, right and wrong is a matter of opinion and a relative thing. If you protect the relationship by being nice, things will right themselves over the long run.

This of course doesn't mean that you should never breathe a word contrary to the views of others, or that you should be a doormat, a hypocrite, or a person without convictions. What it means is that relationships thrive on kindness, support, and harmony. If you want good relationships, avoid arguments, self-righteousness, and trying to prove the other wrong.

A good marriage thrives on unity – not on who is right and who is wrong. In a marriage where there is unity and togetherness, rights and wrongs don't matter much. In a disunited marriage, rights and wrongs don't matter either. In the former, the marriage is going full speed ahead, and in the latter it is falling apart.

THE MIND METER

The social exchange theory says that people are traders at heart. That includes relationships. We keep a mental ledger of rewards, costs, and profits. *Rewards* are anything that we are willing to pay or work for. *Costs* are things that we endeavor to avoid, and *profits* are rewards minus costs. In any situation, as long as the rewards justify the costs the relationship continues.[70]

How do we do our book-keeping? How do we determine the profit-to-loss ratio of every situation? The *mind meter* – a measuring device for everything and everyone – does it for us. The meter constantly measures and gives readings.

In any given day, the meter performs thousands of evaluations – most of them routine and minor, but some of them important. Most evaluations are done in a cursory, instantaneous, and even unconscious manner. In other instances, the meter may spend hours, days, or even longer to give a final reading. These are the complicated cases. A lot of information, both pros and cons, needs be weighed in all sorts of combinations. The meter may keep giving you equivocal evaluations – as is often the case with important matters – and you have to decide what to do.

● *Making decisions*. Let us suppose that you are considering buying a car – a particular car. The meter goes to work immediately. The pluses and minuses line up. Some pluses: "It's a beautiful car. It's about time I got a new car. I love the color, the leather seats, the instrument panels, and the smooth contour. I'll keep it for years, and they'll be trouble-free years." The minuses: "It costs a fortune. It's going to strap me financially. I'll have to borrow money and pay installments for the next 36 months." Then the moment of decision. You ask, "Is it worth it? Do I have to have it and can I afford it?" Depending on the answer, you buy it or walk away from it. Many of the pluses and minuses that enter into any evaluation are unconscious. For instance, you may just decide not to buy the car even when you have ample funds and you really like it. You cannot even understand it yourself, much less are you able to give your reasons to the disappointed salesperson.

● *Relationships*. The good things that you do and say enter the plus bin and the bad ones go into the minus bin of a relationship. A successful relationship has many large pluses and very few minuses.

Couples learn to say good things and do good things to each other. They also manage to avoid hurting each other, for the most part – particularly avoiding the big hurts. Where people fail, however, are the little things – a little nastiness and ridicule here, a little sarcasm and insult there. None of these are really forgotten. They are all recorded and count at every evaluation time. If you are nasty, violent, or unloving in one area of the relationship, it will spill over to other areas. Even those parts of the relationship that are good can go bad.

UNMASKING

Pivotal to a successful marriage is the mutual unmasking of the partners. Early in life we learn to be circumspect in things we say and do. We learn that part of growing up is hiding our feelings – saying things we don't mean, not saying things we do mean, and acting in one way while we really want to act in another. This type of role-playing is useful in many social situations. It can be construed as social sensitivity, for instance. It may provide security by not exposing our secrets – our true thoughts and desires. We fear that if our true inner thoughts were to be revealed we would become vulnerable and we might also hurt others. We fear that others may think less of us if they really knew all about our shortcomings, so we cover and even distort things. All this is often done with the aim of projecting the image of being a worthy – if not perfect – person.

We enter marriage bearing this programmed phoniness. The strategy doesn't work in the intimate context of marriage, but many people have great difficulty getting away from it. Hence there are pretenses, mixed signals, ambiguous hints, vague statements, and long periods of silence. The result is unhappiness, drifting apart, and possibly divorce.

We advise that you be as honest as you can possibly be with your spouse and do it as soon as you can. The unmasking should not be crude or hurt the partner. Some unmasking is potentially hurtful to yourself, your partner or both, and in these instances you must use care, tact, and wisdom in peeling away the layers of the mask. But you must still do it. This is one of the things that makes marriage unique. It is friendship and more; it is an intimacy of mutual and total acceptance. It is in marriage where you are loved for what you actually are and not for what you pretend to be.

Unmasking is particularly difficult when there is a fear of rejection. This is especially true during courtship, where the couple tries to impress each other and hide their flaws. Once they are married, sooner or later these flaws will surface. If the bond is strong enough, the gentle revelation of flaws will do little damage and may even strengthen the relationship. When both of you gradually unmask, you both unload heavy mental suitcases and experience great relief.

What keeps the mask on, in addition to the fear of rejection, is the fear of exploitation. It is foolish to say that keeping the mask on has no redeeming value, or that you should pour out every bit of your inner thoughts and past experiences, that you should reveal every weakness and flaw you might have to the first person who is willing to listen. There are risks, there is a price for unmasking – and it should not be done with anyone and everyone. Self-disclosure provides the other person with intimate knowledge about you. Human beings are not perfect, and this knowledge may be used against you to various degrees – ranging from a little innocent teasing to vicious and vindictive blackmail.

Psychologist Carl Rogers writes:

> Perhaps I can discover and come closer to more of what I really am deep inside – feeling sometimes angry or terrified, sometimes loving and caring, occasionally beautiful and strong or wild and awful – without hiding these feelings from myself. . . . And I am hopeful that I can encourage my partner to follow his or her own road to a unique personhood which I would love to share.[2]

▶ 25 ◀

CHAPTER

PROTECTING YOUR MARRIAGE

A good marriage is like a treasure that must be protected. There are a number of potential threats that can deplete your treasure or rob you of it altogether. It is up to the two of you to safeguard it. The stresses of life are endless, and tension comes from many directions. The news media daily inform us of disasters and misfortunes in places that our great-grandparents hardly knew existed, much less had to concern themselves with; and we must find and expend the energy needed to keep a career on track, meet social obligations, keep up with personal development, perhaps raise children, and deal with many other demands.

It is no wonder that married couples feel besieged and may make a common mistake: that of attributing even outside tensions and troubles to each other and the marriage. Here, we discuss some major sources of threats to marriage and how to guard against them.

AVOIDING THE SPOUSE ABUSE TRAP

The greatest single threat to marriage is the trap of spouse abuse. People must vent their frustrations, anxieties, hurts, and tensions – garbage of the mind must be gotten rid of periodically. There is a tendency to dump this garbage on the nearest or safest person. The marriage partner is usually both the nearest and the safest person. Thus one can easily get into the habit of making the spouse the target of one's hostilities. It's all right to give your partner undeserved credit, but don't give undeserved blame – avoid even deserved blame. Abusing the spouse is bad for the marriage. And what is bad for the marriage is bad for you.

Opportunities for spouse abuse increase when we are frustrated, anxious, or irritable. It doesn't take much to set off accusations and arguments. By misdirecting anger at our spouse, we create trouble in our marriage and a false notion of the sources of our unhappiness – we damage the relationship and may overlook the actual causes of our problems and fail to do something about them. Make it a policy to avoid blaming your spouse under all conditions, particularly when you are overwrought and tired. Try to calm yourself and relax first – a good safeguard against doing rash things that will be regretted later.

"Success has many fathers, but failure is an orphan," is an old saying. In anyone's life there are successes and failures. Studies show that when we succeed we credit ourselves. When we fail, we tend to blame others or the circumstances.[71] In marriage, the spouse is often that convenient target for blame. For example, "Our finances are in ruin, because you spend so much money on your clothes." You must avoid this trap of negative attribution, because it seriously damages the relationship.[72] You must make sure that you give credit to your partner for successes, even when he or she is not directly involved – the exact opposite of scapegoating. For example, think "I got promoted because I have a wonderful supporting spouse who takes care of a lot of things and frees me to spend more time on my job."

HANDLING MARITAL ARGUMENTS

A couple can have occasional arguments – blow off steam, now and then – and still be happy. But when they argue frequently, won't make up afterward, and continue to feel unhappy between fights, there is trouble. This is also true when they never air their differences, never bring up problems, but simply live together in a state of growing unresolved resentment or indifference. Whatever the unhealthy pattern, the time may come when things pile up enough to make the couple think of ending the marriage.

● *Protect the relationship.* The relationship is too precious to be allowed to deteriorate. Remember that you entered marriage with great intentions and expectations. You wanted to make it a fortress for well-being. Don't let it become a fortified prison, and don't allow it to crumble into a useless ruin. Stay with your original goal. Do what it takes to protect it from internal as well as external assaults.

● *Pinpoint the problems.* Even though you may not feel very friendly when you are angry with each other, remember that you are both on the same team – not adversaries. Pool your common energies and resources to destroy the problems, not your marriage. Use the tool of consultation – sit down together and take the time to explore all those likely, unlikely, and even far-fetched reasons why you are feeling the way you do. Write down lists of these reasons, think of as many as you can and maybe find some more.

● *Group the problems.* You may want to group your problems into external and internal stresses. The externals, such as worries about your job, may have internal causes too, such as lack of communication, feeling neglected, and so forth.

Your emotional responses to things as they are brought up will tell you when you're on the track of finding what is troubling you and to what extent. The real problems may be unknown to both of you and they may be buried quite deeply. You need to look carefully for the real culprits. Patiently and together, you can deal with each one and decide on its solution. Communicating your feelings – discussing, talking things over, shedding tears perhaps – you will be bringing things out into the open.

● *Solving problems.* The solution to a problem may simply involve recognizing it, understanding it, and learning to live with it, or getting rid of it altogether – or somewhere in between. In any case, by mapping out the areas in your lives that need attention – and setting attainable goals for improvement – you may be amazed to find that you will feel more in control, more optimistic that tensions can and will be reduced. There can be great relief and healing in just knowing what is bothering each of you as individuals and both of you as a couple.

● *Accepting change.* As couples go through life together, their marriage changes considerably, just as they do themselves. It's almost like having to renegotiate the marriage contract every so often. The couple changes from being newlyweds to being parents of young children, then parents of adolescents. They eventually become middle aged with an 'empty nest' and ultimately, if they are fortunate, elderly. At each stage the strengths and weaknesses of the partners can shift – at one time, the wife needs more emotional support, at another time, the husband needs it.

> Realize that change is a desirable part of life, the spice that keeps us alive and growing. It is not always possible for mates to change together, but it is possible for an understanding spouse to be willing to try to adapt to new situations when they represent needs that are important. By keeping in touch with each other's changing needs, we are better able to wait through periods of change to establish a new status quo, rather than rushing to the conclusion that we are no longer suited to our partners.[73]

HOW TO FIGHT IN MARRIAGE

When you have to argue – and there are times when all couples do – always fight straight and remember the following two points.

● *Remember the goal of the fight.* Why are you fighting? What is it that you want to resolve? Is it worth the fight? Is it about doing dishes, or are you using that as a subterfuge? Keep hidden agendas out of the argument.

● *Use 'I' messages.* Express how you feel and avoid general tirades or accusations of the other person. For instance, say,

"Working all day and having to do all the household chores on top of that makes me furious." Or, "I am angry about this darned long-distance telephone bill – it's a fortune." Avoid saying, "You load me with all the work," or, "You wasted a fortune on that telephone call." The worst fuel for any argument is making it more personal than it has to be.

Three things are essential for healthy resolution of any argument:

- *Understanding the feelings and the problem*. Both of you should understand how your partner feels and what the problem is. For instance, it is clear – in the above example – that your partner is angry and the anger is about the housework or the high telephone bill.
- *Determination to solve the problem*. Having appreciated the feeling and understood the provocation, both of you should solve that particular irritant, perhaps by dividing the housework or allocating a budget for each spouse's long-distance calls.
- *Apologizing and making up*. Apology, particularly when sincere, is an excellent fire extinguisher. The spouse in the wrong should apologize. Even the spouse in the right can apologize to good end. For instance, you can say, "I am sorry I made you angry about this. Nothing is really important enough for me to be nasty to you, honey." This type of graciousness can't help but endear you to your loved one. Apologizing to resolve hurt feelings is a good idea. If it is not done right – when only one party apologizes all the time, or one party takes apology as a sign of weakness – it can backfire.[74] Both of you should apologize – taking turns.

TROUBLED MARRIAGE

Marriage is like a living organism. It can be healthy, beautiful and thriving or ugly and decaying. From time to time even the best of marriages experience illnesses of varying degrees and duration. When people become dissatisfied with a relationship, they may take one of four basic approaches.[75]

- *Voice*. Expressing dissatisfaction, trying to resolve the difficulty, or seeking help from marriage counselors or the clergy.
- *Loyalty*. Remaining passively loyal to the relationship and hoping that the conditions improve.
- *Neglect*. Allowing the relationship to decay and die. Ignoring the partner, refusing to discuss the problem, and letting things fall apart.
- *Exit*. Moving out, or getting divorced.

The first two approaches can potentially save the relationship, while the last two are destructive. There are three considerations that influence the person's choice[76]:

- the degree of satisfaction with the relationship before trouble started;
- the extent of the individual's investment in the relationship;
- the quality of the available alternatives.

THE GREENER GRASS TRAP

In a close relationship such as in marriage, over time the attractive qualities of the partner seem to fade away. You are no longer acutely aware of them. They are there, but subconsciously taken for granted. The bad qualities on the other hand don't seem to fade out so easily and may keep on annoying you. Consequently, a kind of warped picture may emerge, where the partner's faults and flaws are noted while the virtues are hardly seen.

It is this process that plays a major role in making other potential partners look more attractive – their positive features stand out and they skillfully hide their flaws, as required by social etiquette and the desire to make the best impression. Our advice: don't abandon the good deal you have for what seems to be a better deal – the grass is not really greener on the other side.

SOME DO'S AND DON'TS

No marriage is made in heaven – they are all made here on earth by fallible earthlings. So there will be many occasions for disagreements and even heated encounters. But you should expect that anyway. Learning to recognize, tolerate and even appreciate your differences is one of the earliest tasks of the couple. The next step is to develop effective ways of resolving disagreements and defusing potentially explosive situations. All kinds of things work for or against a marriage. Studies show that *defensiveness*, which includes whining; *stubbornness*; and *not communicating* are among the worst, over the long run.[77] There are other things to keep in mind.

● *Don't react irritably to irritability*. Don't get angry just because someone else is. When provoked, or fatigued and stressed, people say things they don't really mean. Permit them to be irritable, without judging or chiding them. Go easy on interrogation and stay calm. Don't immediately demand, "What's wrong?" He or she may not even know. Say instead, "Had a rough day?" Suggest a rest or some food. They will, if not pushed and angered further, usually calm down a bit and reveal what is bothering them.

Sometimes the partner is just plain cranky, and a hug, an apple, or a chance to relax won't help. Then let him or her 'play the tape' and run through the familiar themes of discontent. By not meeting resistance or contentiousness, he or she will soon calm down and feel better. Pre-menstrual syndrome or PMS may affect a wife and it is wise to be aware of the calendar. Also, men can frequently feel upset by mood swings. In both instances, understanding and patience are needed to weather the passing storm.

● *Don't automatically assume that your partner is mad at you.* It may be something at work, or it may be that your spouse is angry about having done something foolish. By not reacting to grouchiness, you will avoid becoming the target of the anger and you will reduce the chances for an argument.

Allow your partner to spout off, and don't try to block the flow of emotions. This is not the time to contradict or disagree with what is being said. Be sympathetic. If your partner has had a bad day, let him or her express it. You need not point out mistakes nor play devil's advocate. You can make hurt feelings much worse by telling what should have been said or done. Don't try to pass off hindsight as foresight and gain a perverted sense of satisfaction and superiority. You should never want to be superior in marriage – always equal.

● *Don't be an adversary*. Spouses hardly need adversaries at home – there are plenty of those in the outside world. Just listen and validate each other's feelings. One does not marry to get a resident adversary, but a staunch ally. Let him or her know you are always on the same side. What else is a spouse for, if not to be a dependable partner to face the world with? You don't necessarily have to approve what he or she did, but you do have to give emotional support.

● *Be positive and supportive*. Even if the comforting partner can see clearly what the situation is, the emotion of the moment frequently calls for being encouraging and supportive. Be a yes man, if at all possible, but you don't have to agree with someone to allow them to have their own opinion and feelings about things. It is not being dishonest to refrain from offering an opposing position. This is simply recognizing that emotional support is one of the most precious things in marriage. And you should provide it. If your partner had wanted 100 percent rationality, he or she would have married the multiplication tables or a computer.

One will never forget how a spouse "always came through for me, through thick or thin" – and the memories will be recalled fondly decades later. The spouse who was "never there for me when I needed it the most" is also remembered.

● *Never criticize*. This is a good maxim for all marriages, but difficult to live up to. It is the pure gold of the relationship. Earlier, we called criticism a psychological ax. It is worth reminding you again to avoid this ax as much as possible. If the partner has made a mistake, or done something wrong, it will become evident during a heart-to-heart talk. There is no need for the one who should give comfort to act like a heavy adviser. Naturally, good advice can be offered during calmer moments, when the spouse is no longer upset and perhaps ready to receive it. Even then, be circumspect and use the gentlest method of delivery.

● *Air your grievance.* Periodically, there might be a legitimate grievance between you. Don't bottle it up, talk about it. Take a walk together or sit down for a cup of tea or coffee. Discuss the complaint and sincerely seek what you need to change or do to redress the grievance. Perhaps a hug and the reassurance of affection is all that is needed. Sometimes a drastic change of habit is required. Whatever it is, don't clam up, sulk, or make general accusations. Be specific. Talk about it and be determined to resolve the problem.

● *Don't mix the difficulty with the person.* One of the hardest lessons to learn is to keep the person and the problem separate. Of course, there are instances where the person is the problem. Even in the majority of these cases you can handle things so that the two are kept separate. For instance, if he or she does something that you don't like, use a team approach. You may want to say, "This particular thing is worrisome. How can we get rid of it?" rather than saying, "This is a terrible habit you have. What are *you* going to do about it?" The approach that separates the person from the problem doesn't threaten or offend. But when you mix the person and the problem – when you attack the problem in this fashion – you are also attacking your partner. For example, your partner likes to have people at the house more often than it suits you. You may say, "If you liked to socialize so much you should have stayed single." This is a sure way of attacking the person rather than the problem. You can say instead, "Socializing is fun. We need to work it out so that we can have our private times as well as time to socialize."

● *A stated grievance is not always the real issue.* A gentle, "What's really bothering you, honey?" often brings to the surface a problem that the partner wasn't even aware that he or she was upset about. It may be a financial difficulty, a speech to give, a report due at the office. This type of background worry is frequently expressed in disguise. The temper fuse gets short, and he or she barks at the slightest provocation.

● *Talk problems out.* Listen sincerely, attentively, and without interruptions. Don't fidget, don't be impatient and don't trivialize. If it is important to her, then it must be important. If he thinks it matters, then it does. Be a fine sounding board – a listener who is not too busy with rebuttals, falsifications and other matters to offer an open ear.

● *Avoid accusations and counter-accusations.* The "you never's" and "you always" are deadly volleys that can sever affectional bonds. Even when you are 100 percent justified in your accusation, the consequence is harmful for the marriage. You can always air grievances without resort to accusations. For instance, you feel that your husband is not doing a certain agreed-upon chore. Instead of accusing him of negligence, you can gently remind him, "Honey, would you remember to do the laundry? We are out of dishtowels."

● *Disagree, but don't disapprove.* Disapproval, particularly when heavy, is crushing to the spirit. It is very threatening to think that you are not any good – you are not liked – or you don't measure up. Self-preservation and self-esteem, in their broadest sense – are extremely important. A natural reaction is to build defenses by retaliating or avoiding the disapproving person. Make sure that your disagreeing is not taken for disapproval.

● *Don't be someone who ferrets out faults.* We are trained by our teachers in school to analyze, to be critical and judgmental and to point out flaws. While these may be useful skills in our occupations, they can be disastrous in marriage, where compassion, human understanding and uncritical love are most needed.

Once you have rationally assessed, chosen and then become permanently committed to your partner in marriage, you should operate under a completely different set of rules that have nothing to do with logical criticism. You need to put aside some of your critical approaches in order to create the kind of loving, accepting atmosphere that allows you to get along with each other.

Spouses are in the day-to-day business of giving loving emotional support. Be analytical and critical with everything else except your partner. You love your partner, remember? And love is beyond the farthest reach of logic.

- *Assume the best intentions, forgive and be patient.* Don't look for trouble. Always give your partner the benefit of the doubt. Take things in the best possible way, even when they are not offered in that spirit. Forgiveness and patience are great virtues that you will want to exercise through the years.
- *Keep the concerns of your married life private.* Neither partner should complain about each other to friends or relatives. This is a form of backbiting and it can cause serious harm to a marriage, because even small quarrels can be blown out of proportion and become major problems when discussed with outsiders. Sympathies may be offered from different sides and hard feelings become exaggerated, positions are taken and must be defended, and reconciliation becomes more difficult.

When you have difficulty working things out between you, then seek the advice of a professional counselor, not the meddling of just anyone who may – intentionally or unintentionally – add fuel to the fire.

- *Don't use the "I told you so" whip.* Much hard feeling is the result of using this painful psychological whip. It is a terrible habit to get into. At every turn reminding the other that you, in your infinite wisdom, foresaw the consequences and gave a warning, but he or she did not heed your wise counsel. No one really needs this treatment – not even children. You should never use whips of any kind, mental or physical. When it is absolutely essential to remind someone of the folly of an action, do it with extreme care so that the person learns without being hurt.

Our base nature derives a perverse satisfaction from seeing another person fall on his or her face. There is a sense of superiority, a self-righteousness, and even sadistic pleasure. But the price for these experiences is unacceptably high. Remember that two people can play this game; best not to play it at all.

- *Be generous with smiling and approving.* The emotional relations between spouses are extremely fluid and can change from moment to moment. A smile or a loving glance at the right time can evaporate ill-feeling in an instant. The couple makes up and the sun begins to shine for them again.

Just as important is active approval. No one – no matter how accomplished – is ever beyond the need for approval and recognition. Approval is as vital as air. So, be on the look out for fanning the relationship by genuine approval.

● *Be sympathetic and empathetic*. In past ages, a husband was thought to need more sympathy and empathy than his wife, because it was assumed that her life somehow was less stressful. It was further assumed that nurturance and care came more naturally to women. Therefore, men implicitly expected to receive this type of special care from their wives as their entitlement. But these are old suppositions that have little relevance to the present age. Working either inside or outside of the home, women are just as stressed as men. Therefore, they are entitled to the same loving understanding and nurturance traditionally reserved for men.

● *Be affectionate*. A daily hug that lasts for a couple of minutes, when arriving home, can work wonders at draining away built-up tensions. Each partner can better handle work problems when reassured by a loving, caring human being. This daily hug is preventive medicine. There are many ways of expressing affection. Just a few examples: Write him a little love note, compose a poem for her, telephone unexpectedly, just to say "I love you."

● *Develop a word trap*. A mental filter that traps every negative word that wants to leave your lips is a marvelous device for use in any relationship. The quality of marriage depends on censoring those words that put your spouse in a bad or hurt mood. Just because you may be in a bad mood, for instance, is no reason for putting your spouse in the same state. Further, when the conversation starts on painful or negative memories and thoughts, it tends to feed on itself and unearth more of the same.

But what about sharing our true feelings with our most intimate friend, our spouse? Well, you have to tread a narrow line – the line that separates legitimate venting from verbal outpouring that creates hurts. We advise you to guard against getting into the habit of voicing every negative thing that comes to mind, if you want a high-quality marriage.

▶ 26 ◀

CHAPTER

ENHANCING MARRIAGE

Even the most successful marriages are not perfect. Perfection is striven for, approximated, but never achieved. This is good news, for it means that marriage can keep getting better and better. It is an investment that, when properly handled, can keep growing. Enhancing marriage requires certain practices that empower the union. Some of them are discussed in this section.

VERBAL NURTURING

Words are important because they contain information, may indicate future action, and influence others. For example, your spouse may be in an agitated mood. You may say, "I think you are worried about the doctor's appointment you have this afternoon." He may smile and say, "You're right. I guess that's what's bothering me – I am afraid she might find something wrong with me." What you did in this case, is that you crystallized the vague agitation into a specific concern. Whether indeed his agitation was wholly or partly due to his upcoming check-up is not important. The important thing is that he – under your influence – attributed his agitation to the impending visit.

Using words, labels, and descriptions is a powerful way of influencing other people's thinking, feelings, and actions. When wisely used, this approach can nurture the positive and destroy or weaken the negative qualities, to the benefit of the relationship.

● *Repairing a flaw*. Suppose that shortly after your marriage your husband says or does something that seems to you to be sexist. The last thing you want to do is to react by saying – even teasingly, much less seriously – "Boy, you sure are quite a sexist. You certainly had me fooled. But now I see that I am married to a genuine, 100 percent sexist male. Deep inside you are like the rest of them." If you say that, you are inadvertently helping him to see himself in that light and accept it. You might crystallize an undesirable quality – sexism – in him. People tend to wear and act out their labels. Additionally, labeling him sexist may free him of any pretense of not being one.

When you treat the instance this way, you box him in with no graceful way out. Now that you "saw him for what he is," he feels free to be what you think he is. The result: you may end up with a licensed and certified sexist husband. As far as he is concerned, this is one thing that he doesn't have to work on, since he is already convicted and sentenced. Additionally, his herd mentality finds a certain pleasurable sense of affinity – by your telling him that he is just like other men. Men want to be like other men, and women want to be like other women.

On the other hand, if you were to respond to what you perceived as sexist by saying something like, "You know, it is so easy to learn prejudice and so hard to get rid of it. We all have to fight those battles all the time. I find myself, from time to time, stereotyping men too. You and I understand the tragedy of this and we must keep on working to get rid of it. You help me and I'll help you."

This latter approach is both honest and wise. It places the problem of sexism out there where the couple can jointly solve it. An added dividend of this waging of a common war is that it brings the couple closer together. As a general rule, the greater the number of challenges and problems that the couple tackles together, the greater is their closeness and feeling of unity.[78]

● *Nurturing a seed.* Using verbal nurturing, you can latch onto the faintest good act or idea and nourish it by elaborating on it and praising it. You can even go as far as pretending that you see something there when it might not really be there. This is not being devious or dishonest, it is a very noble effort at gently planting good seeds and nurturing to fruition those that are already there.

Suppose that in the early days of your life together you notice that your husband clears away his plate after dinner. You are not sure about his next move. Is he going to help with clearing the rest of the table and help with the dishes, or is he going to make a beeline for the easy chair and bury his face in the paper while you do the work of clearing, washing and tidying? The thing to do is to immediately praise him while he is clearing his own plate by saying something like, "One of the things I love about you is that you are such a considerate guy over little things like doing the dishes. It is terrific that we work together and play together." Give him a nice hug and act as if he is going to continue helping with the chores.

By so saying, you capture the germ of a wonderful habit and give substance to something that may not have been there at all until you so wisely created it – the idea that he is a considerate and helpful guy who helps with the chores, the notion that you work together and you play together.

● *People act consistently with their own self-image.* If you help them to see themselves as caring, kind, helpful and loving, people tend to act that way. If you label them otherwise, they also tend to behave accordingly. Hence, verbal nurturing is extremely important in human relationships. This powerful tool has to be used wisely and honestly for the common good. When carelessly used, it can backfire. Use it gently and with great care. It will work wonders for you.

Sometimes people try hard to look good. For instance, trying to appear courageous, generous, lacking in prejudice, and so on. The effort might be very feeble and transparent, but it is foolish to expose them and burst their bubble. This type of action can deal a devastating blow to their fragile effort to become what they are aiming to be.

The thing to do, in these instances, is to rally to their support. Lend them encouragement and strength to keep it up – even when the thing has a grain of pretension in it. It is better to start pretending a good quality than not even attempt it at all. These valiant attempts can be nurtured into the real thing in due course.

LITTLE GIVINGS AND CARINGS

If you want to have an excellent marriage, don't look out for number one – yourself – always look after the number one person in your life – your spouse. Make a commitment to do a lot of little things on a daily basis that please your partner, even at a little cost to yourself.

For instance, quietly do the dishes while she is busy doing something else; switch your plate that has the tender part of the meat with his while he is not looking; sneak some money into his wallet from your own allowance so he can have a little extra; take the less comfortable chair so that she is forced to sit on the more comfortable one. The opportunities for these delicious little bits of unselfishness are only limited by our imagination. You need to do these things discreetly. You should not expect immediate recognition of the kindness and reciprocation of it. If you do, it becomes a calculated barter. Just do it to bring a little extra sunshine into the life of your loved one. In time, your spouse will find out about your endearing actions and will most likely follow your example.

TEASING, JOKING, AND HUMOR

A successful marriage has no room for malicious teasing, and uses jokes carefully – but has a lot of wholesome humor. Shared laughter is magical. It is both a tranquillizer and a stimulant for the soul. Teasing should be avoided – because it may be funny only to one of the pair at the other's expense. Also, no matter how innocently teasing is intended or packaged, it still has elements of hostility, ridicule, and fault-finding. An old saying calls teasing and mockery the sharp scissors that sever friendship.

Joking is all right provided that the jokes are not sexist, racist, or profane. A home without laughter is like a garden without flowers. It is a wonderful thing to be able to laugh – genuine, loud, prolonged laughter. The best kind of humor is that which does not involve having fun at someone else's expense. Ethnic, sexist and personally degrading jokes are little more than disguised insults and hardly require any talent. Remarks that make only demeaning references to other people are a sign of an unimaginative and lazy mind, not of a sense of humor.

RULING OUT DIVORCE

In this age of instability, getting married and divorced is just another social event to many people. "You get into it and see. If it doesn't work, you get out," so goes the attitude. But marriage is not just a social deal consummated on a trial basis. It is an emotional bond of committed love between two human beings and should be lifelong. All the available studies show that divorce is seldom the solution to the interpersonal problems of the couple. We strongly advise against it. It is a very poor method of problem-solving.

- *Divorce, the in-thing?* Some people think that there is nothing wrong with getting divorced – it might even be an 'in-thing,' since many people do it. A myth has been circulating that one out of every two marriages in the U.S.A. end in divorce. This myth started following a 1981 report by the U.S. National Center for Health Statistics, which said that there had been 2.4 million new marriages and 1.2 million divorces during the year. In actuality the 1.2 million divorces were from a pool of 54 million married couples, and that makes the ratio of divorces to enduring marriages far less than one out of every two.[79]
- *The divorce advisers.* Prevalent negative attitudes toward marriage – partly based on faulty data – not only influence the

general public but condition marriage counselors to consider marital misery, despair, and break-down as normal parts of the 'outdated' practice of marriage. Many so-called marriage counselors are really divorce advisers – because they seem bent on mediating divorce, rather than helping to bring about reconciliation.

● *Clearing the air as you go*. Our advice is that you should work things out that threaten your unity as you go along. Don't let them pile up and save them for some never-to-come ideal time for discussion. These little things have a tendency to compound daily and the next thing you know, there will be full-scale fireworks.

● *Ride out the temporary rough spots*. Every marriage has rough periods. Prepare yourself to ride them out. For instance, studies show that satisfaction in marriage is usually high in the beginning, dips as the heavy responsibility of raising children takes its toll, and rises to new heights when this responsibility is over and the couple are alone again.[80] The birth of the first child is a considerable strain on the marriage and additional children add to it. Couples who find themselves estranged while in their thirties are very likely to feel much greater contentment with each other in their forties and thereafter.

Many couples who hang on to their marriages during the hard times – and refuse to succumb to what looks like the easy solution of divorce – eventually find themselves greatly rewarded a few years later when the relationship happily flourishes again. Every marriage can be salvaged, if the partners are determined enough to nurse it back to health.

● *Go for the bird-in-hand*. Before you contemplate divorce as the solution to all your marital arguments, make sure that you don't destroy what good things you have on the assumption that you might do better starting all over with someone else. You will, after all, be taking *yourself* along into a new relationship – there is no way that you can divorce yourself. "We're all of us sentenced to solitary confinement inside our own skins for life," as Tennessee Williams said.

We should not look at our spouse as the cause of our unhappiness, nor should we assume that another person would bring us the contentment that we lack within ourselves. If you feel that your marriage is not going well, this is the time to be as realistic as you possibly can, to strip away fantasies about others and to search deeply in your mind for all the wonderful memories of the good times that you have had together. If you could have had those cherished moments together in the past, then it is possible for you to have them in the future as well.

● *Divorce, a likely loss*. Divorce is seldom the satisfactory solution that it may seem to be. Usually the one who causes the divorce sooner or later regrets it bitterly. The new life usually fails to live up to its rosy promise – it is not trouble-free, nor is it any better than the old one. Any new marriage partner will bring his or her own set of faults and problems that must be worked through. The folly of divorce is demonstrated by statistics that show second marriages are no more likely to be successful than first marriages. They break up with the same or even greater frequency.[19] Reconciliation and re-tying of the original love-bond hold a much greater promise of future happiness.

There is simply too much to lose in a divorce. If there are children, the one who has the custody will usually have many years without the presence of another loving parent to help with the enormous task of raising them. The one who does not have custody of the children will be deprived of the joy of their everyday companionship – and will miss out on the swiftly passing years of childhood. He or she will be unable to give them the daily love and guidance needed from a second parent.

Both partners will lose out on sharing their memories from the years they spent together – those precious memories that can never be re-lived with anyone else. The children may lose the most in a divorce, as they painfully struggle with the trauma of trying to parcel their loyalties between two people who, in their eyes, should have belonged together forever. Speaking of how divorce affected her, a young girl once said, "When my parents were married, it was like having a solid, sturdy floor under my feet. Then suddenly the floor vanished, and I had to cling to the walls with nothing to stand on.

That's what their divorce felt like to me." Studies show that many youngsters suffer for decades from the pain of breakups.[81]

● *Divorce, the court of last resort*. We feel that divorce also has its place. There are instances where nothing else works. When the relationship degenerates to the point of creating lasting repugnance and loathing, only then should ending the marriage be contemplated. But when there is still even a spark of good feeling, the couple can put their marriage back together. All efforts should be made to give the marriage a chance. Always allow for a reasonable cooling and reconciliation period.

● *Marriage matters to others*. Marriage is more than just a contract of convenience between two people. The whole human race has a stake in its survival and success, because the stability of personal relationships affects that of society. The family is at the very foundation of society, and to the extent that it fails, the collective well-being of mankind is jeopardized. We are all deeply affected by the multiplication of unhappiness that divorce inevitably brings to the couple – and the grief that children and other relatives suffer over broken marriages.

▶ 27 ◀

CHAPTER

MARRIAGE BUSTERS

Children, parents, in-laws, other relatives, friends, jobs, financial and social pressures can stress the marriage. These and others are potential marriage busters that you need to know about to protect the marriage.

CHILDREN

Children – your very own – can put the marriage under severe strain. When other strains are added, the union can fall apart. First, there is the unwanted or the unexpected child. That in itself creates tension and problems. Then, there is the child that you wanted to hold your marriage together – that is likely to add to the rough going. Chances for problems sky-rocket when the couple bring children from a previous marriage. Even under the best of circumstances children require an enormous amount of time, as well as psychological and financial outlay.

Human beings, and that includes children, by nature do what they can to maximize their gains and minimize their losses. Rapidly they learn the ropes about doing things that get them what they want. At least for the early years, children are purely self-centered, and are motivated by what we called primitive love.

Driven by short-term self-interest, children adopt special ways of interacting with each parent. Some things they do are not even consciously planned, while others are fully thought out. But all are aimed at serving their own needs and interests – with little regard for anything else. It is this disposition that aims to sweep aside anything that gets in its way, even to the point of instigating fights between the parents and reaping the spoils of the war.

For most part, children do not realize that they are damaging or even destroying the couple's relationship – they don't do it maliciously. But if what they do works, they keep on doing it again and even refine their tactics. For instance, when the parents quarrel or have a falling-out, they may react by becoming more kind and indulgent to the child and spend more time with him and draw closer to him. These actions may be triggered by feelings of guilt. They may feel bad about treating the spouse shoddily, and they try to prove to themselves that they are really very kind and tolerant by excessive kindness toward the child. Or they simply feel in need of affection, acceptance, and sympathy. So they may turn to a readily available surrogate. This type of parental behavior is a potent reinforcer for the child. The child feels that he has that parent as a powerful ally and source of gratification, particularly when the parents fight.

Also, children play off one parent against the other to get special privileges. Their techniques may not be sophisticated – may even be blatant. But they get better at it with age and experience, and they get very good at it if it pays off. Eventually, this type of manipulation takes place even by design and at the conscious level. Children don't care what it is doing to their parents as long as it is playing into their hands and achieving their objectives. Hence, a cardinal rule of any marriage should be the inseparable unity of the husband and wife even regarding their children. The children should never discover the slightest crack in the parents' union. If they do, they are capable of working it into a permanent chasm.

PARENTS, IN-LAWS, RELATIVES AND FRIENDS

It is important to establish sound interpersonal relationships with parents, in-laws and friends, but any of them can harm the marriage, either intentionally or unintentionally. For instance, a father-in-law who never really approved of the marriage; a former boy-friend who still hangs around the old flame; a friend who has found a nice hang-out – one and all are potential troublemakers. It is up to the couple to streamline their relationships with these people in the light of their new life together. And the best time to do it is right away. This is the time when people, including parents, more easily accept the new rules and the sooner you do it the less likely that some undesirable pattern will become established.

Marriage can bring with it significant social pressures. Perhaps you were a free-spirited single person who still lived at the parental home with few social obligations. When you were single, you roamed as you pleased. Now social demands begin to descend upon you. You are invited (read, expected) to do all kinds of volunteer work for the community and the pressure of time begins to mount. There are moments when you long for the freedom of a single person. You keep dreaming about recapturing that life? Forget it, and move on. You are an adult now and there is no going back. Chances are that you wouldn't be happy if you did. So work it out together – again, by consulting on how best you can meet these pressures.

WORK

This is the age of dual-career families. An increasing number of women are finding their way into the higher echelons of the professions. These women have to work even harder than their male counterparts to overcome long-held stereotypes and to succeed in a work environment basically set up for men. An additional pressure comes from domestic chores, which – although they may wait – never go away. What if one or both of you must travel a great deal in connection with your job? Can you afford domestic help? Can you afford not to have it? Is one of you going to have to work nights while the other works days? Can you live with this arrangement, or can it be changed? You should be married to your spouse foremost, not to your job or anything else. Together, you have to take those steps that keep the job-related pressures from wrecking your marriage. You do this by consultation (see Chapter 20). You define your goals and your priorities. The integrity of the relationship should be at the top of your list – together, explore and do what it takes to insure it.

HOUSEHOLD CHORES

No matter how poor or affluent you are and irrespective of your lifestyle, there are always daily chores. You can be flexible and creative and minimize the drudgeries. But, you still will have to do something about shopping, cleaning, cooking, and so forth. You could be asking for trouble if you ignore these chores or make your partner responsible for all of them.

Be smart. Talk things over, make a list, and divide the work right down the middle. From time to time, go over the list again – revise it and work out a new assignment for each. Women do not have a cooking gene nor do men have a gene for repairing the family appliances. If a woman is mechanically inclined, why shouldn't she be the grease monkey of the family? If a man loves to cook, why shouldn't he?

So far as possible, see if you can do the chores together. It is more fun and it gives you more time together. Why not do the laundry or the dishes together, for instance?

BATTLES

To make your relationship into a constant battle is a sure way of destroying it. Yet a successful marriage thrives on free, caring exchanges; differences inevitably arise and must be worked out. Jean and Veryl Rosenbaum, in their book *How to Avoid Divorce*,[27] give excellent advice on this subject. The list below includes some of their ideas on verbal habits you should avoid when discussing problems with your spouse.

- *Ordering or directing*. Expressions such as "you must; you will; you have to."

- *Warning and threatening*. "If you don't, I'll get mad; I'll leave you; I won't speak to you."
- *Preaching and obliging*. "You should know better; you ought to do it; it is your duty to me."
- *Instructing and lecturing*. "Do you realize? Here is why you are wrong; the facts are different."
- *Blaming and name-calling*. "It is all your fault; you're stupid; you are totally wrong."
- *Psychoanalyzing*. "Your real problem is this; your lousy childhood is at the root of your problems; your hidden motive is . . ."
- *Sarcasm*. "Oh, sure; I'll bet; that'll be the day; I'll believe it when I see it."
- *Probing and interrogating*. "Why this and not that? Who can verify what you say? Do you have any proof of that?"
- *Avoiding and shifting*. "Forget it; we'll talk later; let's think about something else; don't waste my time."
- *Flabby language*. "You know what I mean; a word to the wise; you figure it out."
- *Accusing and dead-ending*. "You always do that; I never do this."

TRYING TO CHANGE PEOPLE

Changing people is incredibly difficult. Equally incredible is the way we keep trying to do it. People don't change easily or very much. Marriage should not be a project – a constant campaign of trying to reform and change each other. The following factors work against change.

- *Change requires effort*. The law of conservation of energy rules our life, unless we have overriding reasons to work against it. Changing our ways and habits requires effort, and if the payoff is not there, we won't be motivated to make the effort.
- *Change is disruptive*. Each of us, through a life of experience, learning, and trial and error, puts together a complex personal style. Change, even that which seems minor or easy, involves tinkering with pieces of an elaborate working structure. So it can be disruptive and hence it is resisted.

- *Stability is valued.* Even if a person is willing to invest the necessary energy and put up with the disruptive effects of change, being readily changeable is not necessarily a virtue. We deal with so many different people and situations, and all demand that we change to their specifications. Some of these changes are major and contradictory. No one is capable of meeting these varied demands and still retaining any degree of sanity. There are also other disadvantages in changing too readily. People who do so may be the unsure, unpredictable, or unprincipled. Not being able to change easily is not necessarily bad for a relationship. At least you know where he stands or what she is likely to do. There is stability, consistency, and predictability.

So people resist change. They are at relative peace with themselves, and they have to be. Otherwise they cannot function and they fall apart. From time to time, people may bend a little, change a little, and accommodate something new. Frequently, these changes are in response to specific situations and are only temporary. People tend to revert back – given a chance – to their old ways.

Don't bank too heavily on your ability to change people, particularly adults. Whenever possible, try to change yourself or the situation to improve the relationship. A simple change of expectations will often improve the relationship much better than massive efforts at trying to change the person.

▸ 28 ◂

CHAPTER

MARRIAGE & OTHER PEOPLE

Couples must work hard to build a solid relationship between the two of them. They must also deal with relationships involving parents, in-laws, friends, clubs, charitable and religious organizations, and so forth.

Every activity and relationship is stressful, even when they are pleasant. When they are unpleasant or too numerous, then the stress can become unbearable. Outside demands have a way of piling up and seriously tax the couple. We should regularly examine our activities and make sure that we don't overload ourselves.

When children arrive, for instance, a major reallocation of time and energy is called for. The couple's time together should not be the first to be sacrificed. Some rethinking will be necessary and low-priority outside activities should be the ones to go. Each of us also needs to have personal time – time to be alone – to meditate, read a book, or do whatever is important to us.

PARENTS, IN-LAWS, AND RELATIVES

Life is full of competing demands and conflicting loyalties. There are so many relationships to deal with. In a successful marriage, the relationship between the couple is the most important one – the one that they must protect and nurture before all others. When this primary relationship is firmly established and thriving, the couple can securely attend to the others.

- *Let people know about your priorities*. Make sure that relatives and friends know who is the number-one person in your life – your spouse. By so doing, you discourage attempts by them to compete for your attention or drive a wedge between you.
- *Treat each other with respect*. Both in private and in public. Don't put up a false front – screaming at each other when alone and trying to be civil in the presence of others.
- *Don't complain to others*. Complaining about your spouse to your parents, friends or others is deadly to marriage. If you have a grievance, the one who should know about it is your spouse – the one who has an investment in you and the relationship.

The extended family can be a source of valuable love and support. Yet parents, in-laws, children and relatives can also be mixed blessings. On the positive side, parents, for instance, can be wise friends. They can be a resource for useful advice. The advice you don't like or disagree with shouldn't be a problem. Just listen politely, and in the end do whatever you think best. Parents can generally give you many good tips that come from a lifetime of experience. In them, you can see a model of a couple who has successfully bonded for many years, so they must have done a few things right.

On the negative side, interfering or bossy parents and demanding relatives can be taxing. Meddling parents are particularly troublesome – because it is almost an article of faith that they only want to help. In other instances, parents may take sides with their 'child' and gang up on his or her partner. This is not always done maliciously; for many parents it is simply the exercise of their protective reflex. The results are always the same – undermining the marriage.

There are other things that you need to be aware of in dealing with relatives. Keep the following in mind.

● *Never make a rash commitment.* Commitments should be honored, regardless of to whom they are made. But those made to relatives take on added import. Always ask for time, when presented with a request or a demand. Make it a standing policy that no commitment is ever made without full consultation with your spouse – and with ample time to think about the ramifications. This practice will endear you to your spouse, earn you the respect of others, and forestall rash commitments that you might live to regret.

Consider the case of a man who was visiting his father in a retirement home. The elderly man had a nice private room, his meals were served in a clean and attractive dining room, and all his personal needs were provided for. On impulse, during a visit, the man asked his father to come and live with him – without consulting his wife or thinking through the ramifications. The father accepted on the spot and moved in a few days later. This 'kindness' almost wrecked the marriage on top of alienating the father. His move into the home caused major disruption. Since both the husband and wife worked outside the home, the father was left totally alone all day, and didn't like it. So they got him a dog, and the problems were compounded since the father was less than dependable about taking the dog out when needed. Besides, all the services provided at the retirement home now had to be furnished by the couple themselves. This became a particularly trying ordeal because of the man's special dietary requirements and preferences.

After a few months – and much suffering on everyone's part – the father returned to the retirement home. But the experience left a scar in the relationships – between the father and the couple and between the couple themselves.

● *Beware of kindness.* In dealing with others, particularly older parents and relatives, we are often moved by the noble impulse of kindness – to do nice things for the ones we love or feel sorry for. Remember that any kindness is only kindness at the beginning. After a while it becomes an entitlement in the mind of the receiver. A Chinese proverb says, "You are responsible for the life of the person you save from drowning."

For instance, if you invite a relative to stay with you – out of strict generosity – you had better make it clear whether it is just a week's visit or a permanent arrangement. Something that starts as a voluntary, noble act becomes an obligation. You should know this and also realize that the act of kindness itself is often your sole reward. So, don't expect gratitude and appreciation. And don't plan on terminating the kindness, unless you have made it absolutely clear – at the beginning – that it was only a temporary offer. Otherwise, hard feelings can develop between you.

FRIENDS AND SOCIAL ACTIVITIES

It is good to have friends. In a successful marriage, your spouse is your closest and best friend. A friend is someone you can talk to, you can have fun with, and you can depend on. A good marriage partner is all of the above and more.

Besides your spouse, you can have other friends to enrich your life. Friendship is a bond usually between equals and like-minded persons. In keeping with the new paradigm, an increasing number of men have close friends who are women and vice versa. The friendship of these people is not a sexual relationship. It is based on other attractions that human beings find in each other. Many of these mixed-sex friendships involve happily and faithfully married people who have gone beyond the old mind-set of treating all male–female friendship as inherently sexual.

Most people want friends. This is a legitimate need and marriage should not suppress it. Of course the spouse should be one's best friend, and not necessarily the only friend. But having friends, private or joint, is costly in time, energy, and other resources. You have to work and invest for a thriving friendship. Marriage is a major rearrangement of the network of relationships each of us has. Some old friendships might have to be re-evaluated. You may have to cut back on evenings out with the boys, to give the girl you love what she has married you for. You may have to forgo some of your favorite get-togethers with your friends to spend more time with your husband.

In our view, you should use discretion in your dealings with even your very close friends after you get married. For instance, you should not share with friends your private marriage matters, particularly if your spouse doesn't want them discussed. This type of information is joint property and both parties must consent to its use. More importantly, you should never backbite about your spouse if you value your marriage. Saying negative things about your spouse or marriage is a sure way of destroying the relationship.

The practice of saying bad things about your spouse or marriage is undesirable on at least four counts.

- It will hurt your spouse's feelings when he or she finds out.
- It does not give your partner an opportunity to give his or her side of the story.
- It may force you to behave in ways that would substantiate your allegations. That is, you have to act consistently. If your spouse is behaving badly – as you have alleged – then you are expected to retaliate accordingly.
- It will erode your marital bond.

In addition to friends and relatives, there are religious and charitable organizations, professional societies, and social and recreational activities that demand time and resources. Priorities must be established thoughtfully, as opposed to just taking on more and more until you fall apart under the load. Also, priorities change as we grow older and there must be periodic reassessments to accommodate changing needs and conditions.

Earlier, we advised against making impulsive commitments on the spot, in response to requests or demands from family and relatives. The same rule applies to other people – salesmen, or organizations that use the telephone or computer-generated personalized letters to ask you for something. Don't get pushed into commitments, be it by telephone, by mail, or by visits. In most instances your best bet is to politely, but firmly, say no. In other instances, you can simply say you need time to think about it – you have to check with your wife or husband.

This doesn't mean that you shouldn't contribute your talent, time, and resources to some of the many worthwhile causes that need you. It simply means that you should do it wisely. And, hasty, impulsive decisions are usually prescriptions for regret.

COMBATING IMPOSITION

Each of us faces unlimited demands with limited resources. There are limits to our time, funds, and energy. Like a good manager, we should make best use of our resources to achieve the greatest good. Here are a few things to keep in mind.

- *Make your own decisions and choices*. Of course, in consultation with your life partner – your spouse. Don't allow others to determine what you should do, how much you should give and so forth.
- *Don't over-extend yourself*. Always leave a little margin of safety. Don't over-commit yourself – be it in money, time or whatever – for at least two good reasons. First, if you do, you will deplete and stress yourself. Second, a depleted and stressed person can't be much good to anyone – in fact he or she may become burdensome to others. More important than not over-committing yourself is not committing your spouse to anything without his or her consent.
- *Leave a way out*. Build an escape hatch into every long-term commitment. Take on responsibilities on a trial basis, so that you can have a graceful way out.

For example, you may be asked to serve as a Boy Scout leader. Examine your other commitments, and consult with your wife to make sure that this new activity is something that can be taken on. If the decision is to go ahead, accept it on a trial basis for a fixed time. Then you are going about doing something worthwhile in an intelligent way.

DEALING WITH OLD PARENTS

There are many do's and don'ts when it comes to dealing with aged relatives. As people get old, their health deteriorates, their careers are behind them, their world constricts, and their lives seem spent. The universe of the young child never extends very far beyond himself; gradually, almost everyone learns to become interested in others and other things; then in old age, many people revert to a mind set similar to that of childhood. They become preoccupied with themselves, their health and those things that directly relate to them. Their interest in the outside world diminishes and becomes superficial.

This excessive self-concern is partially justifiable because old age imposes heavy demands on a more and more frail person. But this second childhood is not inevitable. There are many old folks, frail in health and financially strapped, who lead perfectly normal adult lives. Their own resourcefulness, combined with the way they are treated by others – particularly their children – importantly determines the quality of their lives. Their lives, in turn, will impact on those of their children, relatives and friends.

Here are a few tips to keep in mind.

● *Don't make them dependent.* Don't take over their lives, and don't do anything for them that they can do for themselves. Perhaps they do things more slowly or not as well as you do. That's no reason for you to take over. Let them do things and be in charge of their lives.

Let them keep and balance their own checking and savings accounts. They should keep on doing everything that they have been doing all along, for as long as they can. This has at least four advantages: it maintains their confidence in themselves; it keeps them busy doing useful things; it doesn't burden you with chores they can do themselves; and it leaves them less time to complain about real or imaginary problems.

The surest way of landing them in the psychological wheelchair of helplessness is to be overly helpful to them.

● *Don't elicit complaints.* It is a bad idea continually to ask, "how did you sleep last night?" or "how is your back?," or "did you eat properly?," and so forth. People in general – and the elderly in particular – love to tell you all about their troubles. They tell you at length that they didn't sleep a wink last night, that their back is in constant pain, and so forth. You'll never hear the end of it – and you inadvertently encourage complaining by the very fact of asking, which makes talking about their troubles important. Listening to their complaints, you give them the inappropriate attention that they may be seeking, and focus on the negative.

● *Don't reward them for complaining.* It is natural for people to sympathize with the pains, hurts, and sorrows of others – particularly when they are our relatives and friends. This can be the biggest trap.

Whether the person is a parent, a spouse, a child, or a friend, you should never reward them for complaining. When he says, "I don't feel good today. I think that I am coming down with the flu . . ." avoid the wrong move that most people are prone to make. For instance, don't cancel your appointment, stay at home, cook him a delightful soup, and entertain him. Instead, say that he may need to take a couple of aspirins and go to bed. Don't do anything positive that would encourage conscious or unconscious malingering.

Clearly, we are not recommending that you be heartless, insensitive, and non-caring. Not at all. The greater act of kindness to the person you love and yourself is to help him or her to behave in a healthy and responsible manner. You must be very firm in doing all you can to minimize gains from complaints. Instead of falling all over yourself to serve someone who is sick, put things on hold and tell her that things will happen as soon as she gets well. No special soup or attention; special things happen only when someone is not complaining. In short, don't oil the squeaky wheel. Oil it for not squeaking.

● *Don't move to the guilt street.* The guilt street is one of the most crowded and suffocating neighborhoods. Guilt is an agent of control. Many people, particularly the elderly, are experts at using it.

We all have duties of various sorts. The obligation to be kind and caring toward our loved ones is part of the human fabric. Yet kindness should work both ways. You do what you can to help others without going to extremes that begin to cripple your own life. Fight feelings of guilt. Guilt is a reactive and a negative condition. Instead, be proactive and do your kindness out of caring and love and within reason.

● *Help keep them connected.* People thrive on people. We all need people to be with, share with, and talk to, particularly those of our own age and interests. Be a facilitator. See what you can do to arrange for your parent to establish effective friendships. This arrangement is not only good for him or her, it will also free you considerably from playing pal – something that seldom works very well.

● *Help keep them useful.* It makes people feel good when they sense that they are being useful. The trouble is that they are discouraged or they don't know how to make themselves useful. Everyone has a skill they can share; how about tutoring in reading, writing, math, music, arts and crafts, or manual skills – whatever they are good at. If transportation is a problem, students can go to them. There is no shortage of other volunteer work. Give it a little thought and the rewards are well worth the effort. If elderly parents live in the same house with you, make sure that they do a fair share of the chores: cooking, cleaning, doing dishes, mending, dusting, yard work or whatever.

Leading a life of intimacy and sharing that gives real satisfaction to a couple is a difficult but attainable goal. Reaching for that goal is a complex art and science – and relationships with other people are a potential help or hindrance to it. We would like to conclude by saying that the effort that goes into building thriving and healthy relationships with other people is a great investment, but that the relationship between the married couple is the most precious of all; relationships with others, therefore, should be built wisely and be in harmony with the couple's own thriving and eternal bond.

EPILOGUE

In the preceding pages, we have shared with you what we know and how we feel about marriage. We have tried to be objective, relying extensively on facts relating to human nature and how two people can pool their resources for the benefit of both partners. We are convinced that no arrangement can compete with a good lifelong marriage. We are equally convinced that a successful marriage is within the grasp of every couple. Our understanding of what makes for a good marriage is based on input from people in the many workshops and seminars that we have conducted throughout the years; careful study of systematic research by experts; and our own experience of being married for over three decades.

At the heart of a good lifelong marriage is the adoption of a new mind-set – a mind-set anchored firmly in the conviction that the husband and wife are unconditionally equal partners; that the partnership is based on mutual need satisfaction, love, and togetherness; and that like any partnership, marriage requires work. But, unlike other partnerships, only the partners can make it fail.

We have shared with you a great number of do's and don'ts to make your marriage realize its highest potential. But the chances are that you won't be able to practice all our suggestions at all times. We must confess that we, ourselves, have fallen short many times – and we still fall short. But we try hard to learn from our mistakes and minimize actions that might undermine our union. As a result, our marriage has become better day by day and has given us the motivation to keep on trying and to learn as we go along.

All the information in these pages is useful to you, our readers, only to the extent that you use it, and there has to be motivation, a deep desire on your part to improve your partnership. The hard work is up to you – taking the information and applying it, as you see fit, to your own situation. We are interested in your happiness and success in marriage and wish you well. May yours be another instance of successful lifelong marriage, and may you share the joy of being together forever.

REFERENCES

1. Kuhn, T. (1962). *The Structure of Scientific Revolutions*. Chicago: University of Chicago Press.

2. Rogers, C. (1972). *Becoming Partners: Marriage and its Alternatives*. New York: Delecorte Press.

3. Gough, K. (1971). The origin of the family. *Journal of Marriage and the Family*, November, pp. 760–770.

4. Carlson, N. (1992). *Foundations of Physiological Psychology*. (2nd edition), Boston: Allyn and Bacon, Inc.

5. Madden, M.E. (1987). Perceived control and power in marriage: a study of decision making and task performance. *Personality and Social Psychology Bulletin*, 13, 73–82.

6. Browder, S. (1988). Is living together such a good idea? *New Woman*, June, pp. 120, 122, 124.

7. Yllo, K., and Straus, M.A. (1981). Interpersonal violence among married and cohabiting couples. *Family Relations*, 30, 339–347.

8. Kurdek, L.A., and Schmitt, J.P. (1986). Relationship quality of partners in heterosexual married, heterosexual cohabiting, and gay and lesbian relationships. *Journal of Personality and Social Psychology*, 51, 711–720.

9. The U.S. Bureau of the Census (1991). *Statistical Abstract of the United States: 1991* (111th edition), Washington, D.C.

10. House, J.S., Landis, K.R., and Umberson, D. (1988). Social relationships and health. *Science*, 241, 540–545.

11. Adler, T. (1989). Scientists stalk stress–illness link. *The APA Monitor*, 20, 8.

12. Lederer, W.J., and Jackson, D.D. (1968). *The Mirages of Marriage*. New York: W.W. Norton & Co.

13. Livsey, C.G. (1977). *The Marriage Maintenance Manual*. New York: the Dial Press.

14. Wood, W., Rhodes, N., and Whelan, M. (1989). Sex differences in positive well-being: a consideration of emotional style and marital status. *Psychological Bulletin*, 106, pp. 249–264.

15. Khavari, K.A. (1983). Marriage and the nuclear family: a Bahá'í perspective. *Bahá'í Studies Notebook*, III, 63–84; Stewart, T.J., and Bjorksten, O. (1984). Marriage and health. In Nadelson, C. and Polonsky, D.C. (eds.) *Marriage and Divorce*. New York: The Guilford Press, p. 60.

16. Gould, S.J. (1984). Human equality is a contingent fact of history, *Natural History*, November 1984, pp. 26–33.

17. Neimeyer, R.A., Mitchell, K.A. (1988). Similarity and attraction: A longitudinal study. *Journal of Social and Personal Relationships*, 5, 131–148.

18. Straus, M.A., Geller, R.S., and Steinmetz, S.K. (1980). *Behind Closed Doors: Violence in the American Family*. New York: Anchor Books.

19. Cherlin, A. (1987). Remarriage as an incomplete institution, *American Journal of Sociology*, 84.

20. Goldberg, M. (1987). Patterns of disagreement in marriage. *Medical Aspects of Human Sexuality*, 21, 42–52.

21. Givens, D. (1983). *Love Signals: How to Attract a Mate*. New York: Crown.

22. Dion, K., Berscheid, E., and Walser, E. (1972). What is beautiful is good. *Journal of Personality and Social Psychology*, 24, 285–290.

23. Winch, R.F. (1958). *Mate Selection: A Study of Complementary Needs*. New York: Harper and Row.

24. Peck, M.S. (1987). *The Different Drum: Community Making and Peace*. New York: Simon and Schuster.

25. Reis, H.T., Nezlek, J., and Wheeler, L. (1980). Physical attractiveness in social interaction. *Journal of Personality and Social Psychology*, 38, 604–617.

26. White, G.L. (1980). Physical attractiveness and courtship progress. *Journal of Personality and Social Psychology*, 39, 660–668.

27. Rosenbaum, J., and Rosenbaum, V. (1980). *How to Avoid Divorce*. New York: Harper and Row.

28. Khavari, K.A., and Khavari, S.W. (1989). *Creating a Successful Family*. London: Oneworld Publications.

29. Birdwhistell, R. (1970). *Kinesics and Context*. Philadelphia: University of Pennsylvania Press.

30. Archer, D., and Akert, R.M. (1977). Words and everything else: Verbal and nonverbal cues in social interpretation. *Journal of Personality and Social Psychology*, 45, 443–449.

31. Freud, S. (1965). *The Psychopathology of Everyday Life*. New York: W. W. Norton and Company.

32. Tannen, D. (1990) *You Just Don't Understand*. New York: Morrow; White, B.B. (1989). Gender differences in marital communication patterns, *Family Process*, 28, 89–106.

33. Hall, J.A. (1978). Gender effects in decoding nonverbal cues. *Psychological Bulletin*, 85, 845–857.

34. Sullivan, H.A. (1953). *Conceptions of Modern Psychiatry*. New York: W.W. Norton & Company, pp. 42–43.

35. Sternberg, R. J. (1985). The Measure of Love. *Science Digest*, April, pp. 60, 78–79.

36. Gonzales, M.H., Davis, J.M., Loney, G.L., KuKens, C.K., and Junghans, C.M. (1983). Interactional approach to interpersonal attraction. *Journal of Personality and Social Psychology*, 44, 1192–1197.

37. Bouchard, T.J., Jr., Lykken, D.T., McGue, M., Segal, N.L., and Tellegen, A. (1991). Sources of human psychological differences: The Minnesota study of twins reared apart. *Science*, 250, 223–228.

38. Russell, L. (1990). Sex and couples therapy: a method of treatment to enhance physical and emotional intimacy. *Journal of Sex and Marital Therapy*, 16, 11–120.

39. Rust, J., and Golombok, S. (1990). Stress and marital discord: some sex differences. *Stress Medicine*, 6, 25–27.

40. Shedd, C., and Shedd, M. (1980). *How to Stay in Love*. New York: Andrews and McMeel, Inc., p. 12.

41. Moffitt , P.F., Spence, N.D., and Golney, R.D. (1986). Mental health in marriage: the roles of need for affiliation, sensitivity to rejection, and other factors. *Journal of Clinical Psychology*, 42, 68–76.

42. Cosmides, L. (1989). The logic of social exchange: has natural selection shaped how humans reason? Studies with the Wason selection task. *Cognition*, 31, 187–276.

43. Massey, R.F. (1981). *Personality Theories: Comparisons and Syntheses*. New York: D. Van Nostrand Company.

44. Hobfoll, S.E. (1989). Conservation of resources: a new attempt at conceptualizing stress. *American Psychologist*, 44, 513–524.

45. Elliot, G.R., and Eisdorfer, C. (1982). *Stress and Human Health*. New York: Springer.

46. Horvath, S. M., and Bedi, J. F. (1990). Heat, cold, noise, and vibration. *Medical Clinic of North America*, 74, 515–525.

47. Farber, D.F., Khavari, K.A., and Douglass, F.M. (1980). A factor analytic study of reasons for drinking: empirical validation of positive and negative reinforcement dimensions. *Journal of Consulting and Clinical Psychology*, 48, 780–781.

48. Bolger N., DeLongis, A., Kessler, R.C., and Schililing, E.A.

(1989). Effects of daily stress on negative mood. *Journal of Personality and Social Psychology*, 57, 808–818.

49. *Relaxation*. (1985). The United States Public Health publication PHS #1325–85.

50. Mason, J.L. (1985). *Guide to Stress Reduction*. Berkeley, CA: Celestial Arts; Carrington, P. (1978). *Freedom in Meditation*. Garden City, New York: Anchor Press/Doubleday; Bright, D. (1979). *Creative Relaxation*. New York: Harcourt Brace Jovanovich.

51. Benson, H. (1976). *The Relaxation Response*. New York: William Morrow.

52. Pickersgill, M.J., and Beasley, C.I. (1990). Spouses' perception of life events within marriage. *Personality and Individual Differences*, 11, 169–175.

53. Gannon, L. (1981). The psychophysiology of psychosomatic disorders. In S. N. Haynes and L. Gannon (eds.), *Psychosomatic Disorders*. New York: Prager.

54. Garber, J., and Seligman, M.E. (1980). *Human Helplessness: Theory and Applications*. New York: Academic Press.

55. Hocker, L.J., and Wilmot, W.W. (1985). *Interpersonal Conflict* (second ed.). Dubuque, Iowa: Wm C. Brown Publishers.

56. Seligman, M.E.P. (1975). *Helplessness: on Depression, Development, and Death*. San Francisco: Freeman; Schwartz, M. (1978). *Physiological Psychology*. Englewood Cliffs, NJ: Prentice Hall.

57. Cialdini, R.B. (1988). *Influence: Science and Practice*. Boston: Scott, Foresman and Company.

58. Frankl, V.E. (1969). *The Doctor and the Soul*. Harmondsworth, England: Penguin Books, p. 85.

59. Maslow, A. H. (1962). *Toward a Psychology of Being*. Princeton, N.J. : Van Nostrand.

60. Glasser, W. (1984). *Control Theory*. New York: Harper & Row.

61. Ellis, A. (1962). *Reason and Emotion in Psychotherapy*. New York: Lyle; Stuart, M., and Ellis, A. (1980). Overview of the clinical

theory of rational-emotive therapy. In Grieger, R. & Boyd, J. (eds.) *Rational-Emotive Therapy: a Skills-Based Approach*. New York: Van Nostrand Reinhold, pp. 1–31.

62. Kimble, G.A. (1990). Mother nature's bag of tricks is small. *Psychological Science*, 1, pp. 36–42.

63. Khavari, K.A., and Khavari, S.W. (1991). Are human beings too aggressive for world peace? *Viewpoints*, 1, 64–74.

64. Farley, J.E. (1992). *American Social Problems: An Institutional Analysis*. Englewood Cliffs, N.J.: Prentice Hall.

65. Moe, H. (1992). *Make Your Paycheck Last*. Holmen, WI.: Harsand Press.

66. Bandura, A. (1989). Human agency in social cognitive theory *American Psychologist*, 44, 1175-84.

67. Carlsmith, J.M., and Gross, A.E. (1969). Some effects of guilt on compliance. *Journal of Personality and Social Psychology*, 11, 232-239.

68. Bandura, A. (1977). *Social Learning Theory*. Englewood Cliffs, N.J.: Prentice Hall.

69. Shakespeare, W. *As You Like It*, Act II, Scene 7.

70. Beniger, J.R., and Savory, L. (1981). Social exchange: diffusion of a paradigm. *American Sociologist*, 16, 240–250.

71. Weary, G. (1980). Examination of affect and egotism as mediators of bias in causal attributions. *Journal of Personality and Social Psychology*, 38, 384–357.

72. Fincham-Frank, D., and Bradbury, T.N. (1989). The impact of attributions in marriage: an individual difference analysis. *Journal of Social and Personal Relationships*, 6, 69–85; Bradbury, T.N., Fincham-Frank, D. (1990). Attribution in marriage: review and critique. *Psychological Bulletin*, 107, 3–33.

73. Berman, E. (1980). *The New-Fashioned Parent: How to Make Your Family Style Work*. Englewood Cliffs, N.J.: Prentice-Hall, p. 79.

74. Mithcell, C.E. (1989). Effects of apology on marital and family relationships. *Family Therapy*, 16, 283–287.

75. Rusbult, C.E., and Zembrodt, I.M. (1983). Responses to dissatisfaction in romantic involvements: a multidimensional scaling analysis. *Journal of Experimental Social Psychology*, 19, 274–293.

76. Vander Zanden, J.W. (1985). *Social Psychology* (4th ed.). New York: Random House.

77. Gottman, J.M., and Krokoff, L.J. (1989). Marital interaction and satisfaction: a longitudinal view. *Journal of Consulting and Clinical Psychology*, 57, 47–52.

78. The lasting wound of divorce. (1989). *Time*, February 6, p. 61.

79. What's love got to do with it. (1987). *The Milwaukee Journal*, June 29.

80. Marital satisfaction over the life cycle. (1974). *Journal of Marriage and Family*, May, p. 271.

81. Aro, H. (1988). Parental discord and adolescent development. *European Archives of Psychiatry and Neurological Sciences*, 237, 106–111; Runyon, N., and Jackson, P. L. (1987–88). Divorce: its impact on children. *Perspectives in Psychiatric Care*, 24, 101–105.

INDEX